Lunker Lore

Josh Alwine

Copyright © 2017 Josh Alwine

All rights reserved. No part of this publication may be reproduced, distributed, or transmitted in any form or by any means, including photocopying, recording, or other electronic or mechanical methods, without the prior written permission of the author, except in the case of brief quotations embodied in critical reviews and certain other noncommercial uses permitted by copyright law.

ISBN-13: 978-1977635464

DEDICATION

To Addie and Finley. Girls can catch big bass too.

Book cover design and lake map drawings by Jonathan Canny.

jonathancanny@gmail.com

Table of Contents

Introduction   1

Section I - Rarity

Chapter 1   White Whales   3
Chapter 2   The Fish of a Lifetime   12
Chapter 3   The 15lb Club   25
Chapter 4   A Double-Digit Strategy   43

Section II - Public Water

Chapter 5   Public Water Fishing   55
Chapter 6   Night Fishing   76

Section III - Private Water

Chapter 7   Private Water Fishing   106
Chapter 8   La Perla   116
Chapter 9   Camelot Bell   125

Section IV - Chasing Giants

Chapter 10   The Greatest Whopper Ever Told   147
Chapter 11   Big Bass Lessons   171

Acknowledgments   201

Introduction

In early 2016, I published a book entitled *High Percentage Fishing*. In the book, more than 40,000 freshwater data points were statistically examined to establish fishing strategies anglers could employ to put more fish in the boat. Through the application of the knowledge I had gained while writing that book, my catch rates skyrocketed. I went from a few 2-3lb fish per outing to regularly boating 20lb+ five-fish stringers. While these results were fantastic, as time wore on my desire for quality over quantity began to dominate my thoughts. I was catching large numbers of fish, but I also found myself in a seemingly endless cycle of average fish. Frustrated with my results, I conceived the idea to set a goal of catching a 10lb largemouth bass. The goal would be to explore the best public and private fisheries across the country in search of giants.

To be clear to readers, I am not a professional fisherman or a record holder. I am a statistician with a passion for fishing and the good fortune to have some excellent big bass mentors. In writing this book, I have spent countless hours interviewing some of the world's best biologists, trophy anglers, and folks working hard to produce giant bass on private waters. From their collective wisdom, an actionable strategy to catch big bass emerged. It is my sincere hope that regardless of the region of the country you call home, there are tips, tricks, and tactics in this book that will help you target the largest bass in any system. This book is the story of my fishing adventure and a collection of my lessons learned chasing the fish of a lifetime.

Section I

Rarity

White Whales

"Time is probably more generous to an angler than to any other individual. The wind, the sun, the open air, the colors and the smells, the loneliness of the sea or the solitude of the stream, work some kind of magic." – Zane Grey

By most accounts, I'm a young man, advanced in years about half-past thirty. By my reckoning, in fishing years, I am an old man who not for lack of trying is absent the tale of that one great fish. My fish story begins long before my days of chasing green giants in the Deep South. I came close, as it were, to that one fish, in the northern reaches of Minnesota. Some buddies and I, who to varying degrees suffer from much the same fishing addiction, had planned a trip to the Boundary Waters Wilderness Area. The region contains a near endless procession of loosely connected lakes carved from the granite bedrock by enormous glaciers that blanketed the area in the last ice age. Raw and beautiful, these waters are protected by law to keep them that way. The old growth forest that surrounds these lakes are the largest in the eastern half of the United States to remain unlogged. The area is so pristine that drinking water is drawn straight from the lakes. Gasoline motors are prohibited. Canoes are the primary mode of transportation. Help, if it were needed, is often several days of paddling away.

It's against this backdrop that our party set out on a fishing trip early in the new millennium. We were a motley crew of four, and in hindsight quite ill-equipped. We set out for seven days of wilderness camping and fishing in some of the most remote and virgin land that remains in the lower 48. Our trip began on Lake Saganaga near the end of the Gunflint Trail, which itself originates in Grand Marais on the cold shores of the mighty Lake Superior. As we paddled out into the wilderness, our canoes rode low in the water burdened with Duluth packs which carried all our supplies for the week's adventure. To add a splash of excitement to the trip, we intentionally left ourselves a few meals light with the expectation of supplementing our food stores with freshly caught fish. Short on fishing supplies, however, we were not. Every possible fishing scenario had been envisioned and tackle packed just in case. The error of our ways would become painfully apparent as we completed the first of many lengthy and taxing portages.

    Our day one travel plans were ambitious. We planned a 12-hour paddle with a series of brutal overland portages to bury ourselves deep in the wilderness amongst some of the least pressured fisheries in the region. Saganaga is a huge lake dotted with countless islands each virtually indistinguishable from the next. At the time GPS technology was available, but out of range of our collective collegiate budgets. As such we navigated the glacial waters with paper maps and a bit more dead reckoning than was perhaps wise. We soon found ourselves lost in the vastness of the wilderness which had a remarkable degree of sameness in all directions. My group would be ashamed of my confession, but I suspect we pinballed about for the better part of four hours before we serendipitously found American Point, a landmark that finally positioned us. While no one would admit we were lost, we learned our lesson and frequently paused on the remainder of the journey to ensure a true course.

A portage is a trail between two bodies of water that one must traverse when it is not possible or safe to make the trip by canoe. Each man loads himself up with a Duluth pack and whatever else he can carry. There is a rotation of sorts, but a few poor souls wind up with the burdensome task of slinging a canoe over their shoulders for transport. Portages look easy on paper; however, in practice they are tantamount to torture. Measured in lengths denoted in rods (approximately 18 feet), I believe units of misery would be a more accurate expression. In most cases, when two bodies of water are not connected, it is because there is high ground between them. A climb is necessary, and one would think there would be a corresponding descent into the next body of water, but this rarely seems the case. Our first day's travel had three portages. The first was a short distance, perhaps not much more than a hundred yards. The second was considerably longer at nearly a half mile, but not as exhausting as it might have been given a cool breeze, fresh legs, and comparatively flat going. The third and final portage into Esther Lake was a punisher by all accounts. Occurring in the last hours of the journey, we were all tired from a long day's paddle which was made worse by our misadventures following the map. This particular portage was shrouded in dense foliage that would look more at home in the jungles of South America than the Canadian Shield. The temperature had peaked considerably in the afternoon as a warm wayward wind blew in hot humid air from some distant southern origin.

Whether the air dripped with water I can't be certain, but we soon did under the burden of our packs. Ascending a treacherous slope dotted with shapeless masses of granite required periodic leaps across small water-worn gullies which had formed over the years. Adding to our misery was a horde of droning mosquitoes. A local we had met in Grand Marais had jokingly told us the mosquitoes in Minnesota were so big they were the state bird! Between swats I pondered this statement, somehow less funny at the moment, and thought it plausible for a time. After a series of back and forths, no less than three as I recall, we finally slid our canoes back into the water just a short 20-minute paddle from our first campsite on the northern tip of a small island.

When fish are waiting to be caught, setting up camp after a long day's travel is a minimalistic event. A tent goes up, food gets stowed out of the reach of bears, and wood gets gathered for the night's fire. From there, sleek unburdened canoes slide into the water, and the fishing begins. The lake that surrounded our campsite was perhaps a thousand acres, not enormous, but not so small that it could be known in a day. It was comparatively shallow and warm enough that flats near the banks contained many smallmouth dutifully circling beds. Fishing for spawning smallmouth on crystal clear virgin water is more a transactional matter than one of angling skill. Strike rates to well-placed lures approach one hundred percent. It may not be sporting, but for a while it sure is fun. In the waning hour or two of daylight, each adventurer in our group boated fish until his arm was sore. Though tired and worn from the day's trials we ate our evening dinner by a campfire amongst laughter and broad smiles.

In the early morning we broke camp for larger, more remote waters we hoped might hold bigger fish. After an hour's paddle and another portage, the memory of which is still too fresh to write about, we arrived on Knife Lake. We set up camp on a mossy break between two namelessly old boulders each of which were the size of a house. Before heading off for an evening of fishing, we made wagers on the largest fish. The losing boat would be in charge of dinner preparations and clean up.

Opposite camp was a large bay that looked inviting for exploration. My partner and I set off in our canoe with light and quick strokes. Armed with weightless Senkos as lures we hoped to connect with some pre-spawn giants. We found fish immediately, and they were big. The average bronze back topped four pounds, the smallest never below three. For hours we tangled with fish, catching them wherever we laid our lures along the shoreline. Downed logs proved to harbor the larger fish, but in truth they seemed to be everywhere. With the big fish wager on the line, my partner and I labored through vast numbers searching for the one. Then off the edge of a fallen pine, buttressed by ancient glacial rocks, she hit. Smallmouth bass, pound for pound, are the most sporting freshwater fish on the planet. If you've been graced with the good fortune to hook a large one, you know as a matter of personal experience they'll test your gear and angling abilities to the max. This fish, a giant by northern standards, peeled my drag before a series of explosive leaps beautifully silhouetted against a red sun hung low in the evening sky. Once boated she tipped the scales at just north of 5.5lbs and was 22 inches in length. I enjoyed a five-star camp-cooked dinner that night complete with bus service so fantastic that to this day I regularly remind my buddies of their skill.

    In the world of smallmouth fishing 6lbs is widely considered the threshold for trophy class fish. While wanting by some standards, I wound up getting a replica made of that 5.5lb fish as a memento of one of the most enjoyable adventures of my youth. I opened with this story because it highlights one of the most important questions to consider when pondering trophy fishing. Why? A trophy fish after all is a personal and subjective achievement. There is no universal standard. For some, trophy fishing is a means to a mount, a tangible way to document an experience. For others it's an expression of rarity measured in inches and pounds, a currency used to purchase the respect of one's peers. Many view the method and location of the catch to be of paramount importance. The purists amongst us may frown upon fish caught off beds, fish caught from private water, or fish caught with live bait. In fact, throughout this book, these and other controversial tactics will be examined in depth.

****

It is here that'll I'll insert my only caution to the reader regarding the slippery slope of judging the achievements of your fellow anglers. If you find yourself looking down on a method or approach you find less sporting, there may well be others doing the same with yours. As anglers, none of us benefit from this sort of self-righteous thinking. If bed fishing, private water, or fancy equipment somehow detracts from your personal sense of success, then by all means don't do those things. However, if it's legal and a man can look himself in the mirror and be proud of his accomplishment, let your fellow anglers chase their phantoms in whatever way they best see fit. You'll appreciate it when they do the same for you.

****

    I read once that enjoyment comes in four primary forms. The first is relaxing or chemical fun. It can be had easily enough by swinging lazily in a hammock or an afternoon cocktail. This enjoyment, however, is unfulfilling and fleeting. The second form of enjoyment is accommodating fun. This is happiness achieved through social activity such as meeting friends at a ball game or taking your family to a water park. The third type of enjoyment is learning, travel, exploration, and wonder. It's the attainment of knowledge; experiencing the proverbial light bulb moment. The final and most fulfilling form of enjoyment is challenge, mastery, and achievement.

In contemplating this construct of experiences, it struck me that trophy fishing in many ways encompasses all four forms. Fishing at its core is a leisure activity. It regularly occurs as a social sport with friends. Countless hours of research are required to understand the movement and behaviors of fish. And finally, trophy fishing is about possibilities. It's the thrill of the pursuit. The chance to solve a riddle while partaking in a primordial high drama. Perhaps more than anything it is a manifestation of hope and the never-ending conviction that the next cast could be the one.

On a good day, I rise before the sun. I get in a half hour of cardio while absorbing a book. I follow that up with a sit in the sauna, a cold shower, and a healthy breakfast. I toil the day away at work and fill my evening with various obligations. I accomplish what society values. On a great day, I rise with the sun and sputter out on a distant water to meld myself with nature and try to outsmart fish. I achieve what I value, which is arguably nothing more than being.

Someday, I know that taptap on the end of the line will be my date with destiny. That white whale I've been searching for. After a marathon battle she'll roll into my net; then wide-eyed and heart pounding I'll lay her on the tape. Deep down I'll know it's not the fish I'm measuring, but my own will, wit, and fisherman's spirit.

The Fish of a Lifetime

"Fishing provides time to think, and reason not to. If you have the virtue of patience, an hour or two of casting alone is plenty of time to review all you've learned about the grand themes of life. It's time enough to realize that every generalization stands opposed by a mosaic of exceptions, and that the biggest truths are few indeed."
- Carl Safina

Justin Furnace with a Camelot Bell chunker

In early 2016, I had set my goal. I intended to catch a largemouth bass of a lifetime, a double-digit fish. The question this goal begs, of course, is just how difficult is it likely to be? How fast do bass reach 10lbs in size and just how rare is a 10lb fish? What about a 15lber?

Initially, I was curious about what sort of conditions were most conducive to rapid growth in the species. My thought being that the first step to locating a 10lb fish would be to understand the conditions most likely to grow one. As I began to research this topic and speak to several fisheries biologists, I quickly came to know there are two primary genetic strains of largemouth bass; northern-strain and Florida-strain. As the name suggests, Florida-strain bass have a native range that extends through most of Florida and perhaps into Southern Georgia. Regarding growth rates, in the right conditions, Florida-strain largemouth can grow far more rapidly than their northern cousins. I spoke with several biologists who referenced instances of Florida-strain bass reaching 3.5lbs in as little as a year. While exceedingly rare, fish have been documented to cross the 10lb mark in as little as four years. More commonly fish reach this size in 8-10 years. Conversely, northern-strain fish, if they ever reach this size, generally take well over a decade to do so. In one well-documented case in Montana, a tagged 3.5lb fish was caught and determined by biologists to be 19 years old. Regarding top-end size potential, northern-strain fish top out around 15lbs, while Florida-strain bass have exceeded 22lbs. Of course, achieving this growth requires ideal conditions. Florida-strain bass grow optimally in water temperatures in the 70s. Florida-strain bass have high wintertime mortality, which can exceed 80% in waters that drop into the low 40s. This effectively limits their range to waters south of Tennessee. Furthermore, if the water temperatures get above 80 degrees fish can start to suffer from reduced growth due to high metabolic rates. In exceptionally warm environments like Southern Florida, this increased metabolic rate can also significantly shorten the life of the bass. The picture below highlights the difference between the two strains. Both fish were caught in Lake Casitas by big bass angler Tom Young. The top fish, a Florida-strain, weighed in at 18lbs 10 oz. and the bottom fish, a northern-strain of virtually the same length, weighed in at 12lbs 4 oz.

Photo courtesy of Tom Young

In addition to water temperature, the other requirement to grow giant bass is an abundance of prey. To maintain its weight a bass typically needs between five and seven pounds of food for every one pound of body weight. That is to say that if a bass weighs three pounds, it will need roughly 15-21lbs of forage on an annual basis just to hold its three-pound weight. Beyond maintaining its weight, a bass will need an additional 10lbs of edible protein for every one pound of growth. Translating this into more tangible numbers, a bass would have to consume approximately ten thousand average sized threadfin shad to achieve 10lbs of size. Big bass are murderous creatures with voracious appetites. Said simply, for bass to achieve maximum size potential they need Florida-strain genetics, the presence of vast amounts of forage, and moderate water temperatures to give them a long runway of lifespan.

During the process of researching growth rates in bass, it occurred to me that there was very little data available on just how hard it was to catch a largemouth bass of any particular size. I scoured the web but was unable to find, statistically speaking, just how rare bass of certain sizes might be. Being data oriented by nature, this lack of factual information on the subject created a vacuum I couldn't help but attempt to fill. The problem, of course, is that there is no central depository of information that clearly answers this riddle. Having a professional background in Lean Six Sigma and statistics, I was able to dream up an approach that might yield an estimate of rarity. To solve the problem, however, several key variables needed to be assessed:

1. How many largemouth bass of a particular size are caught each year?
2. How many anglers are there and how often do they fish each year?
3. Finally, and perhaps most importantly, where are these fishermen fishing?

As it turns out, the American Sportfishing Association has answered several of these questions for us. This organization periodically compiles a vast database on the number of fishermen by state, the type of fishing in which they partake, and the frequency that they fish. For instance, their data tells us that in 2011 there were more than 27 million freshwater fishermen in the U.S. who on average fish about 1.3 times per month. Furthermore, the data is stratified by state. For example, we can see that in Indiana there are just north of 700,000 freshwater anglers who each spent about 2.2 days per month fishing.

Answering question number one, however, turns out to be the difficult task in this exercise. No large-scale database reliably captures the number and size of largemouth bass caught by anglers. Worse still, fishermen are notorious, shall we politely say, exaggerators. Even if such a database did exist, it would be unverifiable and of little statistical significance. There are, however, smaller organizations, which do record this data and when this information is analyzed using a series of statistical tools, it becomes possible to extrapolate an approximation for the numbers and size of all largemouth bass caught annually in the U.S.

In 2015 *Bassmaster* magazine rated Toledo Bend as the best bass fishery in the world. Toledo Bend is an enormous reservoir, at more than 180,000 acres that straddles the border between Texas and Louisiana. The lake also happens to have a Lunker program that for decades has rewarded anglers with a free fiberglass replication of any bass over 10lbs that is caught on the lake and weighed on a certified scale at a marina with a witness present. This replica incentive roughly amounts to a financial gain of 500 dollars for the lucky fisherman. While we can't be certain that every double-digit fish caught on the lake is recorded, we can be reasonably confident that a significant portion of the true 10lb+ fish are reliably documented. As no information on where or how the fish was caught is required, I suspect few folks would turn down the chance at some recognition and what amounts to a free 500 bucks.

This assumption is the cornerstone of the case I will build for you on the number of trophy class fish caught in the U.S. on an annual basis. We have established that Toledo Bend is one of the best bass lakes in the world as judged by those who know bass. What then does the Toledo Bend data tell us about the number of double-digit bass caught in its vast waters? It turns out that over the last 25 years, the lake has produced on average, about 31 such fish each year. In its best year, which happens to be the 2015-2016 fishing season, the lake produced a record 130+ fish over 10lbs. When I extracted these numbers from the database, I was shocked at how low they were. From guide pictures and Facebook posts, it can be easy to assume 10lbers are quite common. What the data showed, however, is that Toledo Bend; an enormous lake which routinely ranked as one of the best fisheries in the world only produces a few dozen 10lb+ fish each year. In Texas there are perhaps a few other lakes which, in good years, might be able to approach Toledo Bend in double-digit bass production. Lake Fork, Falcon, and Sam Rayburn jump to mind. In the past, Fork may have well exceeded Toledo Bend productivity, but in recent years fishing has slowed. For the sake of argument though, let us assume that each of these lakes produces similarly to Toledo Bend and that each year they yield to anglers one hundred 10lb+ fish. While there are scores of other lakes in Texas, we can be sure most do not produce double-digit fish at the same rate that these lakes do. Some perhaps generate a few dozen, others only a handful. In total, it quickly becomes a stretch to believe that even an enormous reservoir-filled state like Texas produces much more than a 1,000 or so verifiable fish over 10lbs on an annual basis.

In fact, as part of the research in writing this book, I asked this question of several experts. The consensus of the group was that the state likely produced somewhere between 1,000 - 1,500 double-digit fish annually. This number is somewhat larger than my original estimate because many of those asked included the production of private water fisheries. The number of giants these lakes produce is unknowable, but in 2010 *Bassmaster* magazine published data on its own Lunker Club submissions that indicated roughly 30% of the submissions for 10lb+ fish from its readers came from private water.

    The next step in the process was to answer the question, what is the size distribution amongst these 10lb+ fish? That is to say, how rare is a 14lb fish as compared to a 10lb fish? For this exercise, the Toledo Bend Lunker Program data proves invaluable. Its sample size is large enough that it allows the use of statistical tools to create a precise estimate of size distribution amongst fish over 10lbs. It turns out that of the nearly 750 entries, more than half fell between 10 and 11lbs, while only two fish exceeded 15lbs. At a national level, largemouth bass north of 18lbs are exceptionally rare. Given this rarity, these catches are difficult secrets to keep, and as such their frequency is somewhat reliably noted in the record books. Looking at the top 50 largest fish ever landed, and the rate in which they have been caught allows us to use statistical tools to populate the final bit of data needed to fill in the blanks from 15 to 22lbs. From here the size distribution model on the next page makes it possible to determine the number of 10lb fish produced annually in each state based on the record weight for that state. For instance, if Texas with a state record of 18lbs produces between 1,300 and 1,500 10lb+ fish annually, then we can estimate that a state with a similar amount of water and a

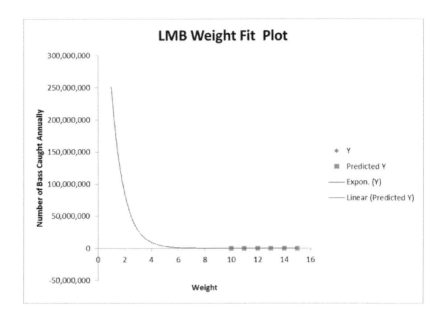

similar sized record fish likely produces a comparable number of double-digit fish. Conversely, a state like Colorado with a state record large mouth of 11lbs 6oz probably produces far fewer 10lb fish. Completing this exercise on a state by state basis allows us to come up with an estimate for the total number of 10lb fish produced annually in the U.S. The final bit of information missing from the model is an overall estimate of the number of bass caught annually. The American Association of Sportfishing does not provide this information, but it does tell us the number of outings per year per angler is roughly 16. We also know that approximately 44% of freshwater fishermen primarily target bass. If we apply this percentage to the number of freshwater outings, we come to 194 million annual outings chasing bass. If we then assume that the average outing yields a catch of three bass, we can then estimate the total number of bass caught annually to be approximately 584 million fish. This figure provides us the final piece of information needed to create a regression model that uses exponential smoothing to surmise the number of fish caught in each weight class 1-22lbs. As an astute reader, it is up to you to assess the assumptions that have gone into this model, but after considerable thought and research, I believe these estimates to be the best that currently exist. They generate a distribution model shown on page 23.

From this information, we can see just exactly how rare each class of fish is by weight. It also allows us to compare how rare these fish are by state, as shown in the chart on page 24.

What the data tells us is that 10lb fish are exceptionally rare. **In fact, across the entire country, the lifetime odds for any given angler catching a 10lb+ fish are roughly 3%.** A fishing "lifetime" has been defined as 16 outings per year for 60 years. Said another way, this means that nationally, out of 100 anglers who fish their entire lives, roughly 3 of them will catch a bass larger than 10lbs. Of course, where you live has an enormous impact on your overall odds. A fisherman residing in Texas has roughly a 33% lifetime chance at a 10lber while the same fisherman in Indiana has only 3% lifetime odds. In any case, 10lb fish are far less common than I ever expected.

As most folks might logically infer, fish become increasingly rare as size goes up. The odds your next cast produces a 10lb fish is roughly 1 in 84,000; the odds your next cast produces a 13lb fish is approximately 1 in 2.5 million. If you're chasing the world record, you would be many times better off trying to win Powerball!

The Double-Digit Mark:

In reviewing the data, I realized the challenge of catching a double-digit fish was going to be far harder to achieve than I had ever imagined. At the time I lived in Texas, and even there, with access to some of the best big bass fishing in the country, the lifetime odds looked long at 33%. Humbled by the data, my past results now came into sharp focus. I knew that if I were going to have any realistic chance of achieving my goal I would have to change my approach dramatically. I needed to stack the odds in my favor by learning every big fish tip, trick, and tactic possible.

Largemouth Bass Catch Distribution

Weight (lbs)	Est. Number Caught Annually	Est. Length	Odds Next Fish Is This Size	Catch Odds Over a Year
0-2lbs	296,071,468	<=13"	1 in 2	24.9
2-3lbs	197,380,979	13"-15"	1 in 3	16.6
3-4lbs	68,062,407	15"-17"	1 in 9	5.7
4-5lbs	17,015,602	17"-19"	1 in 34	1.4
5-6lbs	2,835,934	19"-20"	1 in 206	0.24
6-7lbs	708,983	20"-21"	1 in 825	0.06
7-8lbs	177,246	21"-22"	1 in 3,299	0.01
8-9lbs	61,285	22"-23"	1 in 9,542	0.0052
9-10lbs	21,190	24"	1 in 27,596	0.0018
10-11lbs	6,881	24.5"	1 in 84,970	0.00058
11-12lbs	3,022	25.7"	1 in 193,471	0.00025
12-13lbs	1,224	26.3"	1 in 477,556	0.0001
13-14lbs	232	26.7"	1 in 2,515,126	0.00002
14-15lbs	124	27.5"	1 in 4,715,862	0.00001
15-16lbs	31	28"	1 in 18,863,446	0.0000026
16-17lbs	1.6	28"+	1 in 377,268,920	0.00000013
17-18lbs	1.2	28"+	1 in 471,586,151	0.0000001
18-19lbs	0.9	28"+	1 in 628,781,534	0.000000078
19-20lbs	0.5	28"+	1 in 1,257,563,068	0.000000039
20-21lbs	0.3	28"+	1 in 2,219,228,944	0.000000022
21-22lbs	0.15	28"+	1 in 3,772,689,204	0.000000013
22lbs+	0.03	28"+	1 in 18,863,446,022	0.0000000026

Estimated Lifetime Odds of a 10lb+ Fish By State			
Alabama	13%	Nebraska	0%
Arizona	5%	Nevada	0%
Arkansas	10%	New Hampshire	0%
California	33%	New Jersey	0%
Colorado	0%	New Mexico	5%
Connecticut	0%	New York	0%
Delaware	0%	North Carolina	9%
Florida	33%	North Dakota	0%
Georgia	11%	Ohio	1%
Hawaii	0%	Oklahoma	9%
Idaho	0%	Ontario	0%
Illinois	0%	Oregon	0%
Indiana	3%	Pennsylvania	0%
Iowa	0%	Rhode Island	0%
Kansas	0%	South Carolina	13%
Kentucky	1%	South Dakota	0%
Louisiana	20%	Tennessee	7%
Maine	0%	Texas	33%
Maryland	0%	Utah	0%
Massachusetts	9%	Vermont	0%
Michigan	0%	Virginia	13%
Minnesota	0%	Washington	0%
Mississippi	10%	West Virginia	0%
Missouri	1%	Wisconsin	0%
Montana	0%	Wyoming	0%

The 15lb Club

"The act of fishing – for fish, dreams or whatever magic is available – is enough. It transports us to a special world, and a state of mind, where we are free."
-Fennel Hudson

Dr. Joe Lambert with a Camelot Bell giant

As the statistics of large bass began to soak in my head, their real scarcity was becoming increasingly apparent. Up to this point in my life I had fished across the country and had much success, but none of the fish came close to the 10lb mark. Judging by the number of big bass pictures floating around on the web, I had always assumed not having a trophy had more to do with me than the ghost-like populations of truly trophy bass. Daunting as the task seemed, I can say without hesitation I never contemplated taking up golf. I wanted a double-digit bass.

Einstein said, "The definition of insanity is doing the same thing over and over again and expecting different results." As I thought back over my years of fishing, this notion began to weigh heavily on my mind. These fish had eluded me so far, but rare as they may be, they were out there. I knew I had to change my approach if I wanted to have a real chance at improving my results.

As an avid reader, I bought every book I could find on bass fishing. I scoured the web and soaked up information from every source I could find. The trouble with the literature on fishing is that it is written by fishermen who are notoriously secretive. Yes, I learned many things about the world of big bass, but more often than not the information was generic or based on little more than conjecture. After a few months I had read just about everything under the sun about big bass fishing, but I did not feel any closer to my double-digit goal.

The game changer for me did occur from reading, just not from books on bass fishing. I stumbled across two books in particular that changed my perspective. The first was a book called, *Outliers*, written by Malcolm Gladwell. In the book, Gladwell argues that an individual can master virtually any skill with roughly 10,000 hours of practice. Of course, there isn't anything magical about the number 10,000; this threshold arose as a rule of thumb after studying hundreds of experts and the amount of practice they put into their fields. Initially, I was emboldened by learning this new fact. I just needed to put in 10,000 hours on the water fishing for big bass; I was bound to catch a giant. I have no doubt, had this plan been executed I would have caught a 10lb fish. However, as I began to do the math, I quickly realized 10,000 hours was far more time on the water than I guessed. Some quick division showed that 10,000 hours equaled roughly 3.5 years worth of 8-hour days on the water. Given my busy life, I was lucky if I got to fish a couple of times a month. As I continued to research this subject I came across another book, *Mastery*, written by Robert Green. In Green's book, he emphasizes the importance of mentors. The core concept was that, with the right mentor, in a few hours an individual could absorb what took someone else a lifetime of trial and error to master. Warren Buffett, of Berkshire Hathaway fame, once said that when he was first starting out as a young investor he decided the best way to learn the ropes of the industry would be to find and interview the best investors in the world. Being young and naïve, with a dash of bold, Warren systematically wrote letters to the greatest investors he could find across the country. Surprisingly, virtually all of them agreed to meet with him. He traveled as needed to accommodate the schedules of the executives, and upon completion had met with ten different experts in his field and had an education far better than he could have acquired at any university. The recipe for big bass began to take shape in my mind. I had read the books; I was putting in the practice, now I just needed to find the experts. Taking a page from Buffett, I decided I would locate and reach out to many of the best big bass fishermen I could find. I started with one of my fishing heroes, John Hope.

John is the author of *Trackin' Trophies*, a book which outlines his findings from more than 15 years of detailed observations of large bass in Texas. In the late 1980s he was a fishing guide at Houston County Lake, a 1,500-acre lake in East Texas. As an accomplished big bass angler, he became increasingly interested in the behaviors of big bass. After learning about electronic tracking methods used to track other animals, John got the idea to attempt tracking big bass. Initially, it began half out of curiosity and half as a marketing ploy to drum up business for his guide service. Over the better part of a decade, Hope completed a variety of tracking studies, predominantly in Texas, that focused on the movement and habits of trophy-sized bass. Over the years, dozens of fish were tracked ranging in size from a few pounds to true lunkers upwards of 15lbs. The bodies of water in which John monitored fish ranged from a few hundred acres all the way up to the behemoth Sam Rayburn Reservoir at 114,000 acres. Hope completed the study with astounding persistence. At some points he stayed on the water for days at a time through rain or shine, sleeping in his boat to ensure he captured all movements of the fish. He stuck with the studies through all seasons and water temperatures ranging from 40 degrees to well into the 90s.

    One of the reasons I was so drawn to John as a bass fisherman is that he was one of the few folks who seemed to be applying the scientific method to remove the veil of mystery around big bass. It took me months, but eventually, I was finally able to track him down. For being a well-known name in the fishing world, he was remarkably difficult to locate. As it turns out, John had traded in the lush greenery of east Texas which he had called home for much of his career for the tumbleweeds of west Texas. He still guides, primarily on Amistad and Falcon, but now refers to himself as an on the water coach. He spends time with clients going over bass behavior, looking over maps, and then heading out to the water trying to track down big fish. He also guides regularly for trophy deer and elk on trips as far away as New Zealand.

    After finding his phone number in a remote corner of the web; I gave John a call. I explained I was a fan of his book and asked him if I could drive out to West Texas to meet him. He was agreeable to a meeting but asked what part of the world I called home. When I told him I hung my hat in Houston, he recommended we meet up there, as coincidentally he was planning to be in the area in a few weeks.

I got to meet John on a cloudless day in early April. He was staying at a friend's house and the homeowner had graciously offered to let me swing by. I walked in, introduced myself, and attempted to make a bit of small talk with the man who was nearly two generations my senior. Soon after the conversation started a deep furrow appeared on his brow. I was unsure whether the abrupt shift meant he wanted to get me in and out, or if his mind was just never far from green fish. In hindsight, I know it to be the latter. John started the conversation off talking about funnel points, "A lot of people just don't get the concept of funnel points. Funnel points are just spots where the trail narrows." He motioned to the front entrance of the house and said; "In a perfect world they are no wider than that door. A funnel can be a natural draw, gully, or ditch. It can be a fence row or riprap. It can be a tree line or a creek bed. What they all have in common though is they are identifiable paths that bass use on a daily basis. Big bass are creatures of habit. They get big because they have been successful, and they are not about to change what's worked for them up to this point. With few exceptions, they do the same thing day in and day out." He defined a big bass as 7lbs and larger, and he believed at this size they drastically change their behavior. John said of all the fish he has observed he never saw fish under 7lbs suspending offshore. However, fish over 7lbs all share this common behavior. John hypothesized funnel points corralled big fish into tight areas as they moved around the lake from offshore resting spots to shallow water hunting grounds. Over the years, Hope refined this approach to focus on fishing these funnel points during high percentage times around dawn and dusk, noting that if an angler did this consistently, it would not take him long to land a trophy.

John told me one of the best funnels he had ever come across was an old sunken pond wall that existed on Lake Fork. Before the impoundment of the lake, a backhoe drained the pond by knocking a hole in the wall that was exactly the width of the excavator bucket. Big fish, he said, would suspend out in open water during the day. As dusk approached the fish would follow the pond wall into shallower water and move into their primary feeding area by passing through the cutout. This choke point amounted to a 21-lane highway being narrowed down to a single toll booth! John would stealthily position his boat a short cast from the funnel and keep saturating the area cast after cast. This simple methodology improved his odds of getting his lure in front of a big fish astronomically!

I was fortunate to be able to pore over lake maps with John for hours. We reviewed a half dozen lakes and he coached me on the best funnels in each body of water. Big fish, I learned, will suspend 8-12 feet down out in open water during the day and then follow the draw into their shallow water feeding grounds at night. While funnels can take some effort to locate on topographical maps, with practice, they start to pop out on virtually every lake.

As a final bit of parting advice, John said, "It's also important to remember not all funnels are created equal. Generally speaking, the narrower the funnel the better. Additionally, the best ones terminate in areas that contain structure and cover that create a feeding ground for big bass." Hours later I left John with a handshake of immense gratitude. I had a much better understanding of the first missing piece of my big bass puzzle. Funnel points.

Networked

While John helped me understand some of the high-level concepts for locating big bass and understanding their behavior, Ken Addington took my big bass education to the next level by introducing me to some of the best big bass fishermen in the country.

Ken is not the man you might expect. During one of our early conversations, he told me his story over the phone with his distinctive light and quick southern drawl. Raised in Dallas, Texas, Ken had gotten his start bass fishing as a youngster. By his twenties he was a guide on Lake Fork in the big bass heydays of the late 80s and early 90s. After a few successful years, he decided to trade in the daily grind of guiding for a more stable career in sales.

While Ken had moved on from guiding, he never gave up his pursuit of giants. Extroverted and likable to the extreme, Ken made friends with just about everyone who loved fishing. Over the years, when a big bass was caught on Fork, Ken was often the man holding the fish or patting the back of the man who was.

As time passed, Ken's family got larger, and his available time for fishing started to feel the crunch. Ken began to search for ways to scratch his big fish itch that didn't require 200 days a year on the water. Time and again, no matter where I was in Texas, if I were talking big fish with someone Ken's name would come up. It soon became apparent to me that if there were a shortcut to a double-digit fish, Ken might know the secret. Whether it was my genuine interest in his stories or an irresistible urge to share his passion, Ken agreed to meet me for lunch and share some of his knowledge.

Ken and I settled on a venue during one of his business trips that took him through Houston. When I pulled into the restaurant, I texted Ken and told him I had arrived. Ken quickly responded that he was waiting at the entrance. When I walked in I was expecting to meet a weather-worn, cowboy-hat-wearing, Texas fisherman. To my surprise, Ken was nowhere to be found. I glanced at my phone to check to make sure I was at the right place. Just then I heard, "Hey Josh, it's great to meet you." I looked up and was shocked to see a 6-foot-tall Asian standing in front of me. Ken laughed and said, "Oh yeah,

I forgot to tell you, I'm the tallest Korean in Texas!"

Ken who had been at it for over 40 years had no shortage of Lunker Lore to share. I spent an enjoyable hour and a half that day sitting in a brewery listening to one big bass story after another. As our time ran short at lunch, Ken offered to loop me in with a small group of his friends who had the same passion for chasing giants. He said they all participated in an ongoing group discussion sharing big bass pictures, fishing wisdom, and spent a lot of time talking with the owner of a little known private lake in central Texas. This lake Ken said, "Might be the best bass fishing lake in the world." As we shook hands and parted ways Ken told me to give him a call anytime if I needed advice. He also suggested I go on the Texas Fishing Forum and read the post by a gentleman

Ken Addington with a Camelot Bell 15lber

in the group named Justin Furnace. He said, "Search for the phrase 'nuclear day,' and you'll find it."

That night I remembered Ken's comment about the forum post. After a quick search, I found what he had been referring to. With Justin's permission, I've reprinted his original post here with a few minor edits for clarity. For those uninitiated, what follows is a firsthand account of one of the best days of bass fishing that has ever occurred.

The Nuclear Day

Good afternoon folks-

I debated on whether to chime in at all but was asked to share my story by several friends. I am the blessed angler that caught the 15 ½ pound bass. I want first to say I am not bragging, or trying to sell anyone anything. I am simply sharing my story. I have to believe many of you, just like myself, get on this forum daily hoping to see pics of big fish and read stories about great days. I do not get to fish nearly as much as I would like and live vicariously through this forum most days. I also am not rich; I work 100-hour weeks, and have three young boys at home. I do not even own a boat. I only have a certain budget to fish, and therefore choose my trips to suit my goals. I only share that, to relay the point I'm just an average Joe. I am not a pro, nor am I a great fisherman. I just know there is a lot of controversy over Camelot Bell being a "rich guy's" lake. I probably spend less money on fishing than many on this forum. I have been an avid bass fisherman since I was old enough to hold a pole. That said, I am a trophy bass fisherman. What I mean by that, is that I look for BIG fish. I will fish all day for that one bite. I am not concerned with how many fish I catch. I want THAT fish when I am on the water. As a result of my constant pursuit of giant bass, I only fish in places where I believe my odds are maximized. When it comes to public lakes, I spent most of my time on Falcon and Choke Canyon when they were so good. Nowadays if I am on a public lake, it is usually in Mexico. I usually fish with guides as I do not own a boat currently.

    Here's a brief rundown on my history with Camelot Bell. I had the pleasure of meeting the lake owner, Mr. Mike Frazier, back in 2012. He is a friend of my brothers as they are both in the scientific deer breeding industry. After a couple of phone conversations with Mike, I quickly realized that not only was his lake the real deal but also that he had more passion for growing and catching giant bass than anyone I have ever met. Luckily, he is also a heck of a nice guy, and we have become great friends. This man knows what it takes to grow giant fish, and is happy to share as much of his priceless knowledge as you care to hear. I like catching giants; therefore, I listen. I can tell you that Camelot Bell was built specifically to grow giant fish, and he nurtures it like it is his baby. While Texas Fish and Wildlife would cringe at some of his managing practices, I can tell you first hand that it works. My first trip to the Bell was in March of 2012. At that point in time, it was a trip that I could not have imagined in my wildest dreams. I was with a great friend of mine who is a much better angler than myself. We fished the lake over the course of the two days. The first day our top 5 fish went 52lbs, and on the second day, we wound up north of 54lbs. It took us a while to figure them out, but we did, and it was incredible. We both landed our personal best at that time which was a 12 pounder each. The memories are still vivid.

From here I fast forward to March of 2016. I have learned that weather is very critical to this lake. The fish in this lake are pure Florida's and are therefore very smart and finicky. I knew there was a terrible front coming in and the weather would be going downhill on me as the day progressed. I decided to roll the dice knowing that it would likely be feast or famine. The pressure was dropping, and I thought it might be a special day before the front blew in. I woke up to a steady, pouring rain and stiff 20-25 mph winds. I put on my rain suit, rolled up my sleeves, and went to work. I had caught a 13, an 11, and several other good fish on a particular color of lizard just two weeks prior on another trip to Camelot Bell. This day, they would not touch it. After some experimentation with colors and weights, I finally found what they wanted that day and started catching some fish. Fighting the trolling motor in the wind and blinding rain, I did scratch out a 12, an 11, and couple of other solid fish before the lightning shut me down at about 11:00 am. I had to get off the lake and wait out the heavy thunderstorms until the lightning moved out at about 1:00 pm. Then I got back on and went back to work. I had them figured out at that point. After the heaviest storms had blown through, the fish went into a frenzy. I wound up with 61lbs of fish for my top five that day. I had (6) DD's (double digits). My best 5 being a 15 ½ lbs, 12.5lbs, (2) 11s, and a 10.5lber. What was more amazing to me was that I had behind that best 5, another 10, and (6) 9s. All weighed on highly accurate Boga Grips. I honestly probably threw back some more 9s as it was so silly at that point I was not even weighing fish that I did not think would hit 10lbs. I threw back at least 12 fish that were in the 8-9-pound range. I call this my "nuclear day."

  I will end my novel with the details of my 15 ½ as I know I personally like reading big fish stories. Through the years, I have caught a lot of DD fish off this lake, probably 30ish if I were to give it my best guess. While I have caught a 13 on a chatterbait, and a couple of DD's on a spinnerbait and squarebill, the majority of the big fish on Camelot Bell for me have been on a T-rig soft plastic. The key is usually a VERY slow presentation, with a very light weight pegged with a bobber-stop. This trip was no different until I stuck the big girl. There is a particular area of the lake where the bluegill congregate. While I have always thought that would be the spot to find a giant, I had never even gotten a nibble there until this day. While fishing in the highest winds that morning, I had caught an 11 pounder about 20 yards down the bank from that spot. So on this day, I had a little more confidence in the location. At 3:47 pm, I came down the west bank of the lake, downwind from the spot and made a long cast that landed 18 inches or so from the bank in a little opening in the reeds. Before I could even snap the reel, I knew something special was happening. I must have dropped the lizard on her nose. The instant my lizard hit the water; it was like someone had dropped an anvil from 100 feet in the sky into that exact spot. I swear water exploded 20 feet in the air. My stomach dropped, and I reeled down until I felt weight and set the hook with all I had. To say that she was not a fan of that 7/0 hook going into her head would be an understatement. She literally cut down about 7 feet of reeds as she headed to deep water running horizontally with the shore and off the end of the point. I had the drag cranked all the way down on my Curado, and she was peeling it off; there was nothing I could do to stop her. When I finally got her turned, she came to the top of the water and was sideways to me when I got my first good look at her. My heart was pounding out of my chest. She did get her head out of the water twice but was so fat she could not get her body out. That head shaking at me on both trips to the surface is something I shall not soon forget. Her head was just enormous. After playing her out for about 45 seconds, I finally got her to the boat, and the fella fishing with me got her netted. When that fish hit the boat, I quickly realized I had caught THE fish I have been after my entire life. I can't even remember what all I was spewing at the top of my lungs, but do know I was hoarse the rest of the day. That was the fish of my dreams, and I am grateful that Mike has chosen to share the most special lake in the state. He has graciously offered it up to fishermen like myself to make their dreams come true.

Again, I am not telling this to brag, but just to share a story that I know I would love to see. I hope some of you enjoyed the read.

Have a great Sunday!

-Justin

Justin Furnace with a 15lber

Justin's 61lb stringer is likely the best five fish stringer ever caught in a single day of fishing in Texas. Only a handful of California stringers have topped this number, notably Tom Young's 62.2lbs in 1991 on Lake Casitas, Butch Brown's May 8th, 2010 65lb stringer, which featured an 18.5lb kicker, and Bill Murphy's unbelievable 72lb five fish catch from San Vincent reservoir in 1975.

Immediately after reading his story I tracked down Justin, and in a delightful twist of fate, it turned out he lived less than five miles from my home in Houston, Texas. I met Justin soon after that and was able to talk him into letting me join him for one of his upcoming trips to Camelot Bell. Justin is modest to the extreme about his accomplishments, but for those who know him there is no doubt when it comes to giant largemouth bass he has few peers. He has to his name scores of 10lb+ fish from both public and private waters. While humble in speech, Justin is intimidating in person. My best attempt at a single sentence description would be a thrill-seeking Mr. Clean. Tall and exceptionally fit, Justin speaks about business, life, and big bass fishing with a charisma matched by few. A former personal trainer, drag racer, and construction tycoon, Justin had done more by his 40th birthday than many accomplish in a lifetime. Currently, Justin works an enormous number of hours running a successful concrete company while raising three boys with his wife in Houston, Texas. When he does get a bit of downtime, he spends it trophy bow hunting and chasing the biggest largemouth bass he can find.

In April of 2016, I was just a few short months into my big bass journey. My personal best bass stood at 8lbs, but I had just met two anglers who had successfully boated giants, and they had become my mentors. Like Luke Skywalker under the tutelage of Obi-Wan, I started soaking up everything I could from Ken and Justin. The two also introduced me to their group of fellow trophy anglers which included Dr. Joe Lambert and Mike Frazier, the owner of Camelot Bell. In the coming months, I knew if my phone buzzed there was a good chance it was a message from one of the guys. A big fish had been caught, or some new-found wisdom had been acquired. Later, as I learned more about the group, I realized that these men were some of the best big bass fishermen on the planet and combined, they had boated hundreds of fish over ten pounds. Individually they had each boated 15lbers, putting them in the top one-tenth of one percent of all bass fishermen. They had invited me into their club, the 15lb club, and I desperately wanted to earn my keep.

A Double-Digit Strategy

"It's supposed to be hard. If it weren't hard everyone would do it. It's the hard that makes it great."
– Tom Hanks, *A League of Their Own*

Jack Welch, the former CEO of General Electric, once said, "What is strategy but resource allocation?" The primary resource consumed in the pursuit of big bass is time. The angler's challenge is how best to spend their available time to maximize the odds of catching a trophy class fish. If you happen to be a young trust fund recipient and have no plans but to fish, you can feel free to skip this chapter. For those of you still with me, if you want to succeed and succeed faster, you need to develop a game plan; a double-digit strategy.

Through discussions with my mentors, a roadmap to my future vision of the fish of a lifetime began to take shape. I developed a multi-prong approach that included both private and public water. My ace in the hole for private water was, of course, Justin. My public water plan is summarized below; it contains all the critical steps necessary to stack the odds in the angler's favor:

1. Establish a goal
2. Pick the region and the lake
3. Learn the lake
4. Fish the best times of year
5. Master a few big bass lures
6. Get into and maintain a big bass mindset

The section that follows will flesh out each of these ideas in greater depth. As you read along, I encourage you to walk through the steps mentally. When you complete this chapter, you'll have your double-digit strategy. From there it'll be up to you to execute.

Establish a Goal

Odds are at this point in the book you already know what your goal is. It could be a new personal best. Perhaps it's targeting the largest fish in a system. For me, it was ten pounds or bust. It's important I think, to write this goal down. As you'll see in a later section, perhaps the greatest skill you'll have to cultivate to be successful is stick-to-it-ness, a kind of big bass grit. Losing your way becomes all too easy when you've never defined the destination.

Pick the Region and the Lake

If your goal is targeting the largest bass in a system, you may be comfortable sticking with your home lake. If your goal is like mine, you'll need to consider where you fish carefully. Said simply, if you want to maximize your odds at a giant largemouth bass, you need to be fishing in waters that contain Florida-strain bass. Northern-strain fish do reach 10lbs, but statistically speaking, waters without Florida genetics hold far fewer big fish. I fully believe the strategies outlined in this section will increase your odds no matter where you fish, but to truly maximize your chances you need to be fishing in water where big fish live. Historically speaking, the best three states in the U.S. have been California, Texas, and Florida. As chapter two in this book revealed, in all probability, these three states produce more than 50% of all double-digit bass caught in the nation on an annual basis.

> **Lunker Lore**: Statistically speaking, if you fished a Texas lake during the spring every year for just two days, you would have a higher chance of getting a 10lb fish than in a lifetime spent fishing Indiana.

Lake Selection

Lake selection matters. It's obvious enough, but anglers regularly stack the odds against themselves by selecting lakes based on convenience rather than data-based analysis of which bodies of water are the most likely to produce giant bucket-mouths. The Pareto Principle, developed in the late 1800s, is a mathematical observation that states that in many cases 80% of an effect comes from 20% of the causes. This principle has broad application throughout much of the world in an astounding variety of disciplines. 80% of the land is owned by 20% of the people. 80% of sales are produced by 20% of the customers. You wear 20% of the clothes in your closet 80% of the time. I believe this same principle has significance in the fishing world. 20% of the fishermen catch 80% of the fish. 20% of the water in the lake holds 80% of the fish, and 20% of the lakes produce 80% of the double-digit fish. By this logic, it quickly becomes apparent that to maximize your odds you want to be in the 20%. The right lake. The right spot. With the right knowledge.

In *High Percentage Fishing*, I wrote a piece on lake selection that I still think perfectly outlines the best approach:

Some of the best resources out there are regional fishing forums. To name just a few, in Texas there is: www.texasfishingforum.com; in California www.westernbass.com, and in the Midwest: www.lakelink.com. Virtually every state or region has similar sites where like-minded anglers get together and share information and best practices about fishing in their areas. These sites frequently contain a wealth of information that might otherwise take years to learn. Fishermen, in general, can be secretive, and the sites are not likely to provide you with GPS coordinates of the best spots out there, but the vast majority of participants on these sites are good-natured folks who love talking about their passion. I'd highly encourage High Percentage Fishermen to mine these sites for information pertaining to the best local waters and tactics. You'll quickly learn which local waters are regularly producing big fish and which lakes might be going through a tough cycle. You may even be able to ask questions directly about which waters are best and get answers tailored to the particular type of fish you are seeking (trophy, quality, numbers.) It is also an excellent way to meet potential fishing partners or mentors. If you can find great fishing mentors they may share in a few hours tips and tricks that took them a lifetime to acquire. Now that is a high percentage method!

In selecting a body of water, one of the most important considerations should be the amount of pressure the lake gets. The more fishing and boating pressure, the higher the odds the lake is going to fish tough. Often pressure is a direct function of population density. The closer the proximity to large numbers of people, the higher the probability the lake is going to get a lot of pressure. Google Maps can be a great tool to use to help identify isolated bodies of water that may be off the beaten path but are worthy of additional research. Truly secret lakes probably no longer exist, but it is certainly possible to find low-pressure gems that can yield catch rates far above normal levels for the area. I also use Google Maps to gauge the percentage of shoreline that has been built up for homes and to judge the size and number of boat launches. Obviously, fewer homes generally equates to lower pressure, and boat launches with few parking spaces can lower pressure by reducing accessibility.

    Fishing maps or internet sources may also contain stocking and electric shock studies conducted by the DNR that can also be useful in helping to identify high-potential bodies of water. I was once on a weeklong walleye fishing trip on a large chain of lakes in Northern Wisconsin. After several days of unsuccessful fishing, I was able to use stocking and shock data to determine which lakes on the chain likely had the highest concentration of walleye. This observation helped turn the trip around with several days of excellent fishing! By narrowing down my focus from 20+ lakes to two lakes, I was able to find fish and identify a productive pattern. More importantly, I was able to fish with confidence knowing I was fishing smarter.

Perhaps the only thing I would add to this section would be an emphasis on the importance of hidden gems. In a peak year Toledo Bend, which is regularly rated in the top ten bass lakes in the country, produces roughly 130 10lb fish. At 185,000 acres, on a per acre basis that's one double-digit fish for every 1,423 acres. Conversely, I'm aware of a much smaller lake that only produces roughly four 10lb fish annually. This translates into one double-digit fish per 600 acres or 2.3 times the per acre productivity of Toledo Bend. Furthermore, the fishing pressure on the smaller lake is a fraction of the pressure Toledo Bend receives, and as such, in terms of fishing effort required to catch a 10lb fish, the smaller lake is many orders of magnitude better than its larger more famous cousin!

Lunker Lore: In an upcoming section private bodies of water are explored. Regarding productivity, the best private water can produce double-digit fish at a rate of 1.3 per acre annually. That's roughly 2,000 times more productive than Toledo Bend!

Learn the Lake

In his famous book *The Art of War*, Sun Tzu said, "Victorious forces first achieve victory and then conduct battle. Losing forces first conduct battle and then seek victory." This lesson wrought on the battlefield also has broad application across many aspects of life. The message in short is, do your homework. To be sure, there is no replacement for time on the water, but the value of that time becomes exponentially greater when anglers conduct the appropriate off the water pre-work.

When trying to zero in on the most productive water on a lake, the best place to start is with a topographical map. The rest of this book covers many of the key features you should be looking for in great detail. Non-productive water will be easy to rule out, and funnels, saddles, and other big fish structure will jump out at you. These are the places where you should start your search when on the water. In areas far enough south where ice doesn't form, one of my favorite wintertime activities is scouting a lake. On many occasions I've spent an entire day putting around a lake with my eyes glued to my depth finder without ever making a cast. I'd develop a search plan at home and then use my electronics to search out the spots on the spot. I'm looking for the things you can't learn from a map: rock piles, soft to hard bottom transitions, and cover on the structure. If your target lake is large, and money isn't a constraint, you may be wise to consider hiring a guide. Here again, do your homework and find a guide who is happy to educate. Even if you don't boat a single fish, if you can absorb his on-the-water-experience you can quickly learn big fish haunts that may have taken years to discover otherwise.

Fish the Best Times of Year

Next to fishing the best water, the most important thing you can do to improve your odds of landing a big fish is to focus your efforts during the right times of year. The graph below shows the catch distribution by month of nearly 2,000 bass over 10lbs. In the words of James Carville, "It's the spawn, stupid." Most of the data comes from Texas, Florida, and California, so make adjustments as appropriate given your particular latitude. On any given year, the three to four-month period of the pre-spawn and spawn produces 75% of the big fish caught on an annual basis.

Lunker Lore: Index the chart below to the right by one week for every 125 miles your target lake is north of Dallas, Texas.

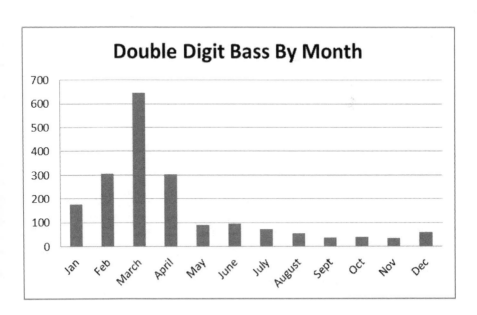

Master a Few Big Bass Lures

One of the biggest mistakes a big bass angler can make is to try throwing everything in his tackle box. A jack of all trades and a master of none is a losing strategy on the water. The graph below has a sample size of over 1,000 10lb+ bass and shows the distribution of the lures used to catch them. The takeaway here is obvious. A few key baits catch a majority of the bass. Later in the book the tactics of exactly how to use several of these lures will be discussed in depth. The particulars of which bait will work best will vary by the lake. Select a few of the top producers and master their presentation.

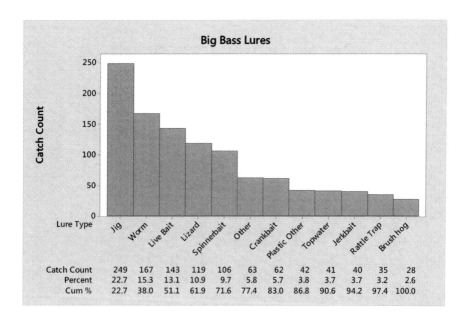

Maintain the Big Bass Mindset

Catching big bass is hard. They are rare fish in any system, and big bass behave so differently from their smaller brethren that they may as well be a different species. Catching them takes a very specific mindset. If you want to increase your odds of catching a giant, you have to be willing to fish differently than you do for catching numbers. This can be incredibly hard because after long hours without a bite the temptation to catch, whatever the size, invariably grows. Ralph Waldo Emerson said, "A great part of courage is the courage of having done a thing before." The same goes for bass fishing. Success will breed more success, but you have to have what it takes to hang in there and hook that first big fish. In the end, your greatest battle may not be with the fish at all, but with yourself and your desire to do the easy thing.

Section II
Public Water Fishing

Public Water Fishing

"The finest gift you can give to any fisherman is to put a good fish back, and who knows if the fish that you caught isn't someone else's gift to you?" -Lee Wulff

Tom Young with a 18lb 10 oz. giant!

In conjunction with my aspirations to fish some of the best private waters in the world, I also began heavily researching just what it might take to join the double-digit club on public waters. In order to maximize my odds, my strategy had developed into a multipronged approach that would focus on public water during the pre-spawn and spawn period, night fishing, and private water bass fisheries. From the data that I had collected and analyzed in my book, *High Percentage Fishing*, I knew that more than 75% of 10lb+ fish were caught from public waters during the spawning season. The reason for this was two-fold. First, fish generally achieve their highest annual weights during the pre-spawn and spawn period. A fish that weighs in at 10lbs from February to March, may only weigh 9lbs the other 10 months of the year. **In fact, statistically speaking, the number of 10lb+ fish in any given body of water roughly doubles during the pre-spawn and spawn period.** Secondly, and perhaps most significantly, the spawn period is the time of the year that big fish are most susceptible to anglers. As I learned from John Hope, throughout most of the year big fish spend the bulk of daylight hours in a negative feeding mode, suspended offshore, essentially uncatchable. During the spawn however, biology shifts the advantage into the angler's corner. The urge to pack on pounds to support egg growth and the need to seek out a spawning bed drives big fish into the shallows. There are thousands of approaches anglers can and do use to catch big fish every year. This section will not attempt to cover all these approaches, but it will highlight a few strategies that I believe maximizes an angler's odds specifically during the pre-spawn and spawning period.

Where

Once an angler has selected a lake which contains an appreciable population of ten pounders, the next task becomes selecting areas within the lake which will maximize the angler's odds of crossing paths with a giant. Funnels are perhaps the single best approach to a trophy, but outside of this tactic there are other methods and strategies which are also worth exploring.

Pre-Spawn Hot Spots

The pre-spawn period typically occurs in water temperatures between 48-60 degrees Fahrenheit. Warming springtime waters begin to drive physiological changes in big bass that force the fish toward shallow water. This time period which can last anywhere from a few weeks to a couple of months often produces some of the biggest fish caught annually.

Pre-spawn fishing for giant bass, particularly early in the year, often requires fishermen to slow down and pick apart structure. It's extremely important for anglers to complete their homework prior to arriving on the lake; in the pre-spawn location rules. In this section we will examine three pre-spot hot spots that will help anglers key in on small areas within a lake that can maximize their chances at the fish of a lifetime.

Points

Virtually all fishermen understand that points create underwater structure that attract fish. In regards to big fish this is particularly true during the pre-spawn period. Early in the season main lake and secondary points serve as an intermediate hunting ground between wintering locations and spring spawning flats. That said, not all points are made equal. The next page shows an example of a fantastic point on Sam Rayburn in Texas that produced a 13lb fish in February of 2016. Let's examine what makes a spot like this so great. First, the spot sits on the northern shore of the lake. In the spring, this water catches more of the sun which hangs low in the southern sky and warms faster. The point is also well positioned to benefit from warm southern winds which will move warm surface water over the point. These two factors combined can lead to water that is several degrees warmer in the early spring than much of the surrounding lake making it an ideal early season location. Secondly, the point is perfectly positioned between shallow water spawning flats and a nearby deep-water sanctuary for giants to suspend while not actively feeding.

Lunker Lore: The spot on the following page is located at: (31° 14.083'N 94° 17.515'W). Use the Navionics boating app to find this spot an examine the nuances that make it great.

The Home of a 13lber

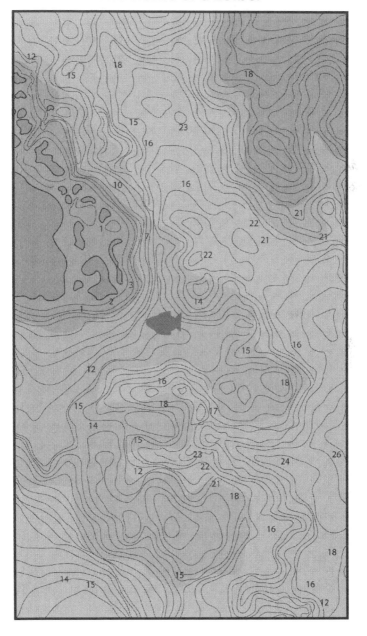

Going from good to great, there is a funnel that creates a highway for big bass to quickly move up into 8-12 foot feeding flats on the point.

Once a spot like this is discovered on a topographical map, the key then becomes finding the spot on the spot most likely to hold giant fish. Use your depth finder to locate these areas. The best spots will have hard bottoms, small rock piles, shell beds, and spotty or non-existent weed cover. Densely weeded areas are difficult to fish, reduce the feeding efficiency of predators, and are generally shunned by giant bass. Statistically speaking the best lures for this time of year tend to be jigs, plastic worms, and crankbaits.

Bridges

Like the proverbial troll, giant bass often make their home around bridges. In fact, the largest bass caught in recent history, which tied George Perry's World Record bass of 22lbs 4oz. was caught in 2009 under a bridge by Manabu Kurita on Lake Biwa in Japan. These locations can make ideal habitat that perfectly balance structure, cover, and forage. Bridges are often located at natural choke down points in lakes that can corral baitfish into small areas as they are moved about by wind-driven currents. Generally spanning both shallow and deep water, the pilings themselves create excellent year-round ambush points. Near the shore, riprap is often present creating further hunting and spawning grounds. Many bridges can be such ideal habitat that large bass can meet all of its yearly biological needs while never needing to move more than a few yards.

The first few pilings near shore tend to hold the most bass; however, big fish can be present anywhere near the structure. Prior to fishing a bridge, conduct a full sweep of the area with your electronics using side scan to note which pilings seem to be holding the most baitfish. The best locations often change based on wind and water conditions, but generally speaking, a few small areas of the bridge will hold the lion's share of the bait. The depth of the bait will dictate the best approach for fishing a bridge. Bait concentrations near the shoreline or shallow water pilings can often be effectively fished with jigs or other plastics. Offshore or deep-water bait may require deep diving crankbaits to reach the most desired areas. Alabama rigs, where legal, can also be lethal. Near deep water pilings these lures can be counted down to virtually any depth and be presented as a tantalizing school of passing baitfish.

On an interesting side note, Manabu's fish was caught on a live bluegill. Indeed, bridge fishermen targeting crappie accidentally hook some of the largest bass taken annually. These fishermen will be reeling in a crappie, often on ultra-light equipment, when their rods buckle over as a giant bass swallows the crappie whole.

Lunker Lore: Rainbow Road, 35°07'20.4"N 135°55'51.1"E

Saddles/Feeding Benches

One of the more impressive big fish strategies I've come across over the years I learned from California big bass fisherman Tom Young. Tom is one of the old grey beards in California who has been targeting huge bass since the introduction of the Florida-strain fish in the 1950s. Tom's resume of big bass is matched by few and includes single fish catches of: 19.3lbs, Lake Castaic, 1993; 18.6lbs, Lake Casitas, 1981; 17.6lbs, 17.4lbs, Castaic, 1991; 17.4lbs, Casitas, 1988. In total he has 58 bass over 15lbs, and 300+ bass over 10lbs. Making Tom's accomplishment even more astounding is the fact that he eschews live bait and bed fishing. Tom is a jig fisherman. I ran across Tom on the web in my research for this book and was fortunate to discuss with him many of the secrets of his success. Perhaps most notable amongst Tom's strategies was his preference for targeting feeding benches. A feeding bench or saddle is essentially an underwater lake structure where a narrow strip of lake bottom rises out of the depths. The image on the next page is based off a sketch Tom provided. It displays a feeding bench he believed could produce a new world record largemouth. Tom pursued just such a giant in the mid-1990s on this exact spot on a western reservoir he denoted only as Lake X. In California the best known of these benches get pounded by big bass anglers from January through May and have produced many of the top 25 largest bass ever caught in the state. Tom believes finding similar, but less conspicuous, structures may be the key to a truly giant bass.

Tom Young's World Record Bench

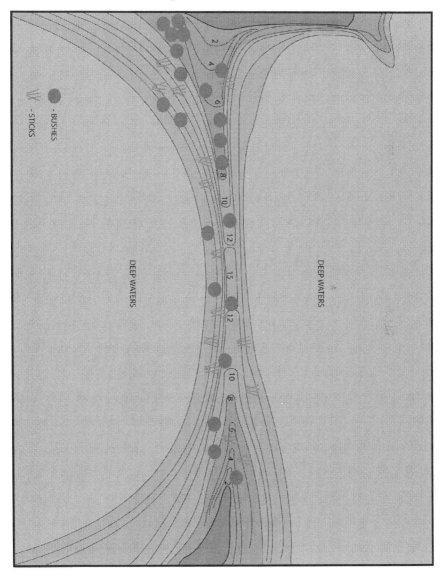

The best benches are immediately adjacent to deep water, are constructed of a hard bottom, and also contain various forms of intermittent cover to attract a sustainable baitfish population. Tom's strategy for fishing these structures is the opposite of most anglers. He positions his boat in shallow water and then makes long casts into deeper water. He then works the lure back to the boat uphill. This approach he says, presents lures in a fashion the fish are not used to seeing. In an article he wrote for In-Fisherman in the 1990s, Tom further emphasized the importance of long casts to effectively cover water without spooking big fish.

> Long casts allow for fishing areas thoroughly without anchoring or waiting for fish to move up. The key again is being quiet, using no electronics that might spook bass, and moving slowly to make multiple casts across an area from different angles-up and downhill as well as across. Keep your boat as far from the target structure as possible. Check the area with a graph only as you leave. A long cast is 75 to over 100 feet. Once the jig is on the bottom, slowly swim or crawl the jig back by turning your reel one-half to one turn, then letting the jig fall to the bottom. Repeat this retrieve until the jig is past the structure or near the boat. The lure should always be within six inches of bottom. Strikes range from a hard thump to only line vibration, line movement, or a loss of feel. A slight tick is the most common sensation.

In the same article, he offered this advice in finding

big bass structures:

> A major point that intersects a baitfish migration route is the best location to fish for giant bass. The point should have deep water (30 feet or more) surrounding it and a variety of structural features that hold baitfish and allow bass easy egress to rocky transitions, gullies, saddles, flats, or humps. One way to find these areas is to start at a dam and stop to fish the first major point you find. With long casts, you should be able to fish every major point in a small lake within a week. And you'll have a good chance to catch a giant bass as you learn the structure.

Benches are not unique to California. Comparable structures exist in many lakes all across the country. Anglers are well advised to follow Tom's advice for locating big bass structures on their home lakes and fishing them aggressively during the pre-spawn period.

Lunker Lore: Tom states that he has caught many bass up to 12lbs on jigs with plastic trailers, but that every bass he has caught above 15lbs has only bit a hair jig with a pork trailer.

Spawning Flats

Bass are remarkably resilient when it comes to their ability to spawn in a wide variety of freshwater environments. Spawning depths can range anywhere from 1 foot to more than 12 feet. Even the timing of the spawn can vary wildly with some fish spawning in waters as cool as 55 degrees and others waiting until water temperatures reach well into the 70s. Beds are virtually always made on hard or sandy bottoms. However, they can sometimes be found on a hard bottom oasis in an otherwise densely weeded or mucky area. On any given lake the majority of fish spawn in similar environments. If you can locate one group of beds, savvy fishermen can then use topographical maps to key in on other areas of the lake with similar structural layouts. Furthermore, fishermen should understand that no law book governs spawning location. Bass can spawn just about anywhere where water temperature and light levels are conducive to successful reproduction. Big bass have been known to spawn on offshore humps that rise out of the abyss into the 5-12 foot range and still others have been seen spawning in the crowns of submerged treetops miles from the nearest shoreline.

Perhaps the best big bass spawn strategy is simply attempting to stack large numbers in your favor. This can be achieved by specifically targeting lakes with high populations of big bass, water visibility exceeding 2 feet, and searching immense amounts of water looking for huge fish. To break this strategy down more specifically let's consider a typical southern reservoir in March.

Step 1: Identify water temperature in the northern, middle, and southern stretches of the lake. In most reservoirs, the north end will warm the quickest, but also contain water with the lowest visibility. Middle portions will contain cooler water but increased visibility, and southern ends near the dams contain the coolest water with the greatest visibility. To justify the time, effort, and expense of a large-scale search water temperatures should be at least 58 degrees in your target area.

Step 2: Check the water visibility in each of the three sections listed in step one. To efficiently search large amounts of water for big fish, you have to be able to see the fish. Anglers vary in their ability to spot fish based on their knowledge of the lake and overall experience, but generally speaking, water with visibility less than 2 feet creates a difficult environment to conduct an effective search.

Step 3: Stop into your local bait shop and try to get a feel for where the majority of fishermen spend their time during the spawn. Often certain portions of lakes are far more accessible than others. This could be due to the locations of convenient boat launches or proximity to areas well known to have produced big fish in the past. As general advice, it's best to avoid these areas as they are likely to get picked over quickly by fishermen.

Step 4: Spend time reviewing satellite images. Look for areas on the body of water that have fewer shoreline homes and greater distances from popular launch sites. The highest use launch sites are often those that are the closest and most easily accessible from the nearest population centers. For most folks, convenience trumps fishing potential.

Step 5: Once you've identified an area that has water temps greater than 58 degrees, water visibility more than two feet, and low fishing pressure, the next task becomes locating likely spawning areas. Start with a detailed topographical map and look for large flats with water depths in the 2-6 foot range. Many bodies of water will have miles of shoreline that fit this bill. From there rank each flat in order of potential, giving added preference to those flats that have deep water access within 100 yards.

Step 6: The next step is to create a scouting plan that maximizes your time on the water. Create a sequence to visit each of the potential areas throughout the planned fishing day. Look at the weather report and try to make sure you are visiting the regions with the highest potential at times when visibility is likely to be the greatest (sunny/low wind).

Step 7: Before you launch your boat you need to make a mental commitment to yourself. Decide that you are looking only for trophy class fish and that you will resist the temptation to stop and fish beds that don't meet your criterion. The biggest bass on a lake may only be on a bed anywhere from a few hours to a few days. Your odds of not finding these ghosts increases dramatically if you allow yourself to get sucked into bed fishing every five pounder you come across.

Step 8: Start the search! If you are fishing during the middle of the week or early in the spawning season, often the best tactic can be to put your trolling motor on the highest setting at which you can effectively scan the water. Follow your plan and do not stop until you find a giant! I cannot emphasize how important it is to stick to your plan. If it's not a trophy fish, keep moving. The name of the game is to cover as much prime spawning habitat as possible. Most fishermen look for spawning beds in water 1-3 feet deep. If you are fishing the weekend or more pressured water, you may have to slow down and search for beds in slightly deeper water. Depending on the water clarity this depth can vary, but it's often 4-8 feet, and the key is to learn to see beds others anglers overlook. It has been my experience that these deeper, harder to see beds often hold larger bass. Studies have shown many bass spawn in virtually the exact same location year after year. Bass that spawn in deeper water are harder to locate and thus have a lower fishing mortality rate than fish that spawn in shallower water. This increases their longevity and thus enhances their likelihood of attaining larger sizes. Keep a close eye on water temperatures as you conduct your search. If water temperatures in the morning are in the upper 50s and fish are not on beds, it may be wise to return to your best areas later in the afternoon. The fish may have pushed up if water temperatures have increased over the course of the day.

> **Lunker Lore**: A great pair of polarized sunglasses is indispensable during the search for spawning fish. For most freshwater situations copper tends to be the best all-around lens color for searching for beds.

Step 9: Catch the fish!

Additional Tips

-Once a giant fish is located, the next task becomes assessing where the fish is in the spawn cycle and how pressured the fish has likely been. This is instrumental in determining a strategy to maximize your odds of being able to catch a giant bass off a bed. The tighter the fish holds to bed, the higher the probability you will be able to catch her. Fish that spook off the bed and leave for extended periods can be extremely tough to hook. It's at this point that fishermen need to analyze the situation to create a spawn profile for the bass which will help dictate the best strategy for catching the fish. One of the first steps is to attempt to guess how long the fish has been on the bed. If you are early in the spawning season, fishing mid-week, or fishing a bed you know most anglers will have overlooked, there's an excellent chance you are targeting a fresh fish. Conversely, if water temperatures are well in the 60s, you are fishing a weekend, or the fish is in shallow or unusually clear water, the fish has likely been targeted previously. The more fishing pressure a bass receives, the more difficult they become to catch. For a truly big fish, this may not matter as a solid effort is in order, but the freshness of the fish and the overall conditions will dictate which tactics are most likely to yield a fish in the boat.

-Before your first cast, observe the bed for several minutes to ascertain which areas of the bed the female tends to favor and note whether a male is present. Often the biggest females will not pull up on beds without a male. If the male is present, go to great lengths to avoid catching him. If you do catch the male, and it's legal to do so, it is wise to put him in the live well until you are done fishing for the female. Hooked fish can release a stress hormone that shuts down the bite on other fish. The mechanics of this phenomenon are not entirely understood, but I firmly believe you significantly reduce your odds of hooking the female by immediately releasing a previously caught male.

-Lure choice for spawning fish matters very little. That said, in most cases you'll want a weighted soft plastic. Jigs or baits with pegged bullet weights provide the most control, but freely moving weights rigged Texas style can make an extra sound which can trigger more bites. I've found that compact lures that hide the hook will often get hit much faster than lures with exposed hooks. Additionally, large baits such as ribbon worms may well trigger bites, but wary fish may repeatedly pick the lure up by the tail well away from the hook making them impossible to catch. All this said, aggressive bass holding tight to the bed will hit a variety of lures. If this is the case, I'll often fish high visibility lures such as white creature baits with the hook embedded into the lure. This makes your lure essentially weedless and easy to see in the water. For finicky fish, more natural colors may be required.

-Once you've selected a lure, cast well past the bed. Work

the bait up to the back of the bed carefully watching how the fish responds. It's essential to move the lure as slowly as possible through the bed. Very often there will be a small golf ball sized spot within each bed that is of particular importance to the fish. Lures outside this spot may be completely ignored; however, a lure sitting on this favored location may be aggressively attacked. If such a spot is discovered, often the best tactic is to simply let your bait sit on this spot and jiggle your rod with almost slack line. Avoid reeling at all at this point. Many reels will take up as much as two feet of line with a single crank. The spot on the spot in a bed is typically only a matter of inches. Find it and maximize your lure soak time in this location.

-Study the behavior of the fish. Some fish will attack a well-positioned lure while it's stationary. Others can be triggered with a hopping motion. Still others, will be driven to bite a jiggling lure. I've hooked fish with lures that sat still on a bed for several minutes.

-If the bed does not seem to have a spot of particular sensitivity, the next tactic is to attempt to agitate the fish into a reaction bite. Cast your lure past the bed, and then bring the lure in at such an angle so as to make contact with the bass center mass in the front 1/3 of the fish. This contact, whether a slow drag or a pop, will often trigger the fish to spin on the lure and attack. It's critical that this tactic only be done with lures that do not have exposed hooks. Exposed hooks could lead to a snagged fish.

Snagging is illegal in most states, significantly increases the probability of severely injuring the fish, and frankly is unethical. Repeating this method will often work an otherwise uncatchable fish into a fit of rage that will eventually result in a bite.

-If these methods fail, in all probability the fish is either not locked on the bed or has been extremely pressured. At this point an angler's best bet is often to leave the area and return later, or to back way off the bed and make blind casts to the area. If you've located an unusually large fish, one of the best methods to mark the area is with a buoy, or if the water is shallow enough, with an orange driveway marker. Position the buoy or driveway marker on the back left or right of the bed and then pull several hundred yards off the bed and allow the fish to rest for an extended period. Depending on how tightly the fish was holding to the bed, this period could range from a few minutes to a few hours. When you return to the fish stay nearly a full cast length away from the bed. Using the marker as your guide make casts well past the fish and work a lure through the area. It's important to maintain constant contact with your bait throughout the cast. Bites can be difficult to detect and often come in the form of a fish picking up a lure, moving in your direction, and knocking slack into your retrieve. Set the hook!

-The last tool in the angler's belt becomes changing lures. In one case on Lake Fork, my good friend and expert bass angler Logan McKenzie spent hours targeting an exceptionally finicky bed fish he believed pushed 12lbs. He tried every lure in his box before finally tying on a giant worm that exceeded 12" in length. The fish immediately hit. Sadly, the story ended badly with his 65lb braid breaking on the hookset.

-When targeting trophy class bed fish, I recommend 12-17lb fluorocarbon line depending on water clarity and how pressured you believe the fish to be. On highly stained waters anglers may well be able to get away with braid and thus dramatically increase their chances of successfully landing a hooked fish. After Logan's story, it probably goes without saying that you should regularly check your line for nicks, kinks, or abrasion.

Live Bait

No review of big bass fishing on public waters could be complete without discussing the use of live bait. While viewed by some as less sporting, live bait fishing is a powerful big fish tactic that few fully master. Choosing to ignore live bait fishing is of course the prerogative of the fisherman, but anglers should know doing so on a wholesale basis may well cost them the biggest fish of their lives.

A common misconception is that live bait always out-produces artificial lures. Quite to the contrary, I believe artificial lures out-produce live bait in a majority of the environments fishermen typically encounter. Artificial lures are versatile and can be fished in virtually any environment. Live bait on the other hand is effective in a comparatively narrow set of conditions. Live bait does its best in well lit, high visibility, relatively open areas. Nature has built into prey a natural instinct to hide from predators. If you put live bait into thick cover it will be quite capable of burying into the cover and summarily fouling your line. Furthermore, most species will attempt to be as quiet and discrete as possible in their movements making them difficult or impossible to locate in low visibility environments. Artificial lures on the other hand can be outfitted with any variety of blades, rattles, and colors to attract bass. Lastly, most live bait must be fished slowly to keep the bait alive. This makes searching large areas for active fish difficult.

So, what then are the ideal conditions in which to leverage live bait to increase your odds of catching a giant bass? I believe live bait, specifically crawfish, shine in the pre-spawn period. Points, funnels, and feeding benches outlined earlier in the chapter all create great locations in which to use live bait. The key is being confident the site contains big bass, and that the area is relatively open.

The subject of live bait tactics is so expansive that it could easily fill an entire book. For those readers interested in learning more, I would recommend they start with Bill Murphy's book, *In Pursuit of Giant Bass*.

Night Fishing

"The secret to fishing after dark is that there is no secret. It's exactly like fishing during the day; only it's dark."
– Jeff Van Remortel

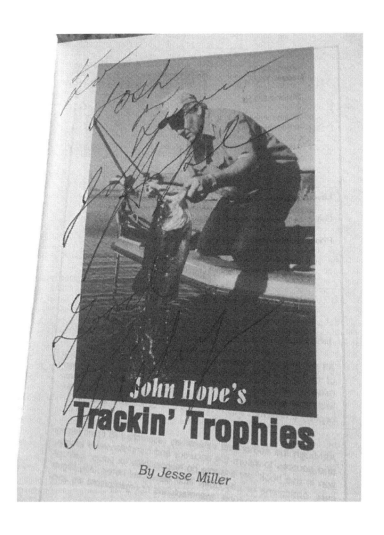

It was a warm evening in June. I had arrived at the lake with just an hour of light to spare. I had recently been turned on to the big fish potential of night fishing, and I wanted to test a concept called Funnel Fishing. For a week I had scoured topographical maps and had picked out the perfect funnel on one of my favorite lakes. Before I headed to my spot, I couldn't help but chase a few fish in my favorite honey holes. I cast my crankbait as the sun sank red and low. I hooked a 3lb fish just where I knew she'd be. Clouds were sparse and thin. The water so closely resembled glass that the reflection created made a seamless transition between the surface and sky. Herons waded shallow, searching for a last morsel in the day's fading light. A frog began its nightly courtship call and was soon joined by an invisible host. Just then another fish. Her splashes broke the stillness of the water. A 4lb dandy.

I soaked in the moment, then collected myself and refocused my thoughts on my quest. If my new fishing tips from John Hope were correct, big fish were waking from their daytime slumber and beginning to move. In much the same way as a hunter might hang a tree stand along a well-known trail, I needed to set up position. My night hunt was about to begin. I motored over to my pre-selected spot, a funnel which deadened into a long rocky berm. I used a two-anchor system; one off the front and another off the back. I pulled the ropes tight to keep the boat motionless and perpendicular to the draw. The moon was nearing full and had just come up as the sun gave up its final color. The brightest of the stars appeared as I made my first casts along the underwater ditch where I hoped a giant largemouth would soon be traversing.

As twilight encroached small waves rolled across the lake as the last boats of the day made their way back to the dock. My lure of choice for the night was a black and blue jig. I made a cast and slowly worked the lure back over the course of a few minutes. A crank or two of the reel, then a long pause. All the while I kept my fingers in constant contact with the line feeling for the slightest twitch to indicate a fish had picked up the lure.

On perhaps the third cast, little more than halfway to the boat, I felt the strike and my lure raced toward the berm. With a sharp hook set and a short but fierce fight, I landed a 5lb bass. A beautiful fish to be sure, but not the class I was after. I cast again as a slight wind out of the south began to pick up. A ripple appeared on the water, and it scattered moonlight like a kaleidoscope. Almost hypnotic in form, at that moment the sensation of being alive was so intense that it quelled any small quiet fears of a synthetic reality; no illusion could be so grand.

As the night carried on a strange gray drapery replaced the distant shoreline. The fog was moving closer when she bit. It was the faintest of taps, perhaps nothing, but hook sets being free, I reared back with a forceful yank that vanished into the weighty parabolic bend of my rod. My drag sang as I fought to keep her from the rocks. A powerful run was thwarted, and then another. Spent, she rolled on the surface and glided through moonlit water toward the boat. She bumped the scale at 8lbs 2 ounces, the largest fish I had ever boated at night. A gem of a fish made all the more special because she appeared when she was supposed to.

Whether she was the biggest fish on the trail that night I'll never know. A fog dense enough to swim through rolled in. I called it a night and made a long dangerous idle, assisted by the guidance of GPS, back to the launch. It was a short evening but it produced one of my largest bass to date. Night fishing, I had learned, is perhaps the last untapped big fish strategy available to exploit on public water.

Night Fishing

One of the key lessons of *High Percentage Fishing* was that fishing pressure has a far greater impact on catch rates than virtually any other natural phenomena. If you take this finding to heart you may well be led to night fishing. Regarding public water, I firmly believe there is nothing better you can do to improve your odds of catching a trophy class fish than to fish at night. The only caveat being that night fishing is *hard*. Ken Addington has never been a fan of night fishing. He's told me a dozen times, "The good Lord made the night for two things, and fishing ain't one of them." Half joking, Ken's issue with the night has nothing to do with the quality of the fishing, and everything to do with the difficulty of the matter. Humans are not well equipped to fish in low light. In addition to the extra difficulty and danger of fishing at night, the change in schedule is more than most can handle. It is, however, precisely these challenges that lower the pressure and allow night fishing to be so productive. If you can master the strategies outlined in this chapter you'll have learned some fundamental Lunker Lore that will enable you to dominate the night bite.

Fish Behavior at Night

In 2016 I had the great fortune to meet one of my fishing heroes, John Hope. John is the author of *Trackin' Trophies*, a book which outlines his findings from more than 15 years of detailed observations of giant bass in Texas. One of John's key findings was that every fish he studied over 7lbs primarily fed at night. The fish would suspend during the day over open water on the first drop off from their primary feeding ground. John called this area their bedroom. As sunset rolled around these fish would become active and move in toward their hunting grounds. They would then spend much of the night feeding. As sunrise approached the fish would once again return to their offshore haunts and remain inactive for most of the day. In addition to this finding John also made several other critical observations:

> -Big fish have preferred depth ranges. Ranges were labeled as shallow (0-8 feet), mid-layer (8-12 feet), and deep layer (12+ feet). No fish in the study had a feeding range that varied by more than 10 feet. Mid-range and deep-water fish only ventured to shallower waters when biology dictated they do so during the

spawn. The mid-range held the most big bass, as they benefited from the best combination of access to forage and reduced fishing pressure.

-Big fish have small ranges. Once a fish reaches 7lbs or so it establishes a home range and a preferred depth. Outside of the spawn big fish rarely leave their preferred range and depth layer. Hope stated big fish had ranges that were typically located close to their spawning flats and rarely exceeded more than a few hundred yards in size.

-Big fish were highly predictable in that they precisely followed a daily routine.

-All large bass Hope studied were predominately nocturnal feeders. They occasionally fed during the day, but only when they were unsuccessful in satiating their appetite at night.

-Large fish are difficult to catch not because they reside in ultra-secretive hard to reach spots, but because they are suspended and are inactive for large portions of the day when most anglers are fishing.

-Hope said, "Fishing pressure eliminates trophy bass in shallow water. Anglers do not allow very many of them to get to be trophy size. In my opinion, if a fish lives in shallow water and manages to reach six or seven pounds, the fishing pressure and boating pressure alone make it move out and become a mid-layer bass."

When John mentioned that every fish he had tracked over 7lbs fed almost exclusively at night, he had my attention. I began to ask him detailed questions about his approach to night fishing. John told me, "One of the first things you need to understand is that big fish are like bulldogs. They are loners. They aren't out there sitting in a pack. These fish don't ambush feed like a small bass. At night they move in and they flush feed through intimidation." I asked John to explain further what he meant by flush feeding. He went on to tell me that during his many night dives he learned that small fish primarily hugged the lake bottom. John said, "Bream are scattered like rocks all across the bottom of the lake." While John never explained why this was, I suspect it is a safety strategy employed by smaller fish to limit the angles of attack by larger predator fish. John continued, "These big bass, they move in following their trails, and they swim around, just as fast as you might go with a trolling motor. They spook these smaller fish, and with a sweep of their tail they are on them. Back and forth they'll go over their hunting grounds, generally in two-hour increments, followed by periodic rest. In this way they will flush feed all night." I asked John whether the bass had difficulty hunting at night. John said, "They have minimal trouble feeding at night. However, they are not perfectly efficient. On any given night they have roughly a 25% chance of having consumed an insufficient amount of prey. If not for this fact few big fish would ever be caught during daylight hours outside of the spawn."

While John's studies took place primarily in Texas, I believe his observations hold true for largemouth in most fertile freshwater lakes. John observed that most fish underwent a dramatic change at around the 7lb mark, transitioning from daytime feeders to nighttime feeders. I don't believe there is anything magical about 7lbs. I believe that on the lakes where he completed his studies this weight marked the minimum size that a bass needed to achieve to lose its instinctual fear of being eaten. On the lakes John studied these fish were likely in the top 5% weight wise of all the bass in the lake. Achieving this size may well flip a switch in the bass's brain allowing them to suspend, without fear, in daylight over open water and to preferentially flush feed at night. In more northern lakes, achieving this top-tier size percentile occurs at much lower weights. That is to say, a largemouth bass in Illinois may well become predominately nocturnal at a weight much lower than 7lbs.

> **Lunker Lore:** John says the ideal depth to target in the summer is 8 feet. In the wintertime the 12 foot mark is preferred. Topographical programs like Navionics allow users to highlight specific depth ranges. Highlight the 8-12 foot range on your favorite lake and look for funnels that intersect cover!

Where to Fish

The simplest advice for locating fish at night is to fish the same spots you would during the day. In this section I'll break out the season's specific locations, but you'll notice that for the most part, they follow the same patterns you'd fish in daylight. If you follow this methodology you will catch fish. You will likely even catch big fish, but there are more sophisticated strategies explored in the following sections that will dramatically increase your odds of encountering a trophy.

> **Lunker Lore**: The local community hot spots, even those called out on popular topographical maps, may receive too much pressure during the day to consistently produce fish. However, these same locations may be dynamite at night when the fishing pressure vanishes.

Lakes

The first critical factor in setting yourself up for lunker success while night fishing is lake selection. If the lake has bass in it fish can be caught at night. However, some fisheries are more prolific producers of nighttime giants than others. One of the best overall indicators as to how well a lake is likely to fish at night is water clarity. Bass can hunt successfully in even the murkiest of water, but your odds of connecting with one at night are directly related to their ability to detect and strike your lure. The lower the visibility in a given lake, the harder that task becomes. While I have caught bass at night in lakes with visibility as low as a few inches, as a general rule of thumb seek out water with at least two feet of visibility. Some of the best nighttime fisheries are extremely clear and highly pressured bodies of water. All the better if these lakes see enormous amounts of daytime pleasure boat traffic. The chaos during the day can leave these lakes as hidden gems to be discovered at night.

Lighted Structures

Lighted structures on the water come in two primary forms. The first is traditional pier lights, and the second is underwater lights. Both can become nighttime hot spots. Pier lights attract insects and other small prey in the lit water below. This sets off a chain reaction in the food chain that ultimately attracts apex predators like bass. These lights are easy enough to locate but are often passed up by anglers for this very reason. Never pass one up without at least a few exploratory casts.

Underwater lights can be even more productive than pier lights. The locations of these lights are often highly guarded secrets. The lights are installed by homeowners who wish to attract fish to their docks for nighttime fishing. Anglers who fish them regularly note that on any given night an underwater light may or may not hold bass. On larger lakes many of the best nighttime anglers will have milk runs where they repeatedly visit as many as a dozen lights over the course of a night. Some nights the lights never hold fish at any point, other nights they can be barren early and stacked with fish late. The pattern can seem whimsical, but when the stars align these areas can load up monsters in impressive numbers! One such night resulted in the stringer of a lifetime for a Texas angler on Lake Fork, whose top 5 fish went for 55lbs with a 14lber as big bass.

As these lights are not on during the day they can be tough to locate. Obviously at night they are easier to spot, but even so anglers often need to be nearby to discover them. Adding to the difficulty the lights may not be turned on every night. However, with the appropriate time investment, dedicated anglers can find these hot spots which have the potential to yield incredible stringers for years to come.

> **Lunker Lore**: Focus on halo areas around lights. This is where bass will primarily hunt. Faster moving lures such as crankbaits can often trigger the most strikes, but crawling plastics across the bottom is the preferred presentation for the biggest bass.

Dominant Big Fish Strategy: Funnel Points

Perhaps the greatest lesson I learned from John Hope was the importance of funnel points. John believed that one of the best approaches to catching big bass was to target them at narrow draws during high probability feeding times.

Page 88 shows a classic example of a funnel from Toledo Bend. Big fish will suspend 8-12 feet down out in open water during the day and then follow the funnel into their shallow water feeding grounds at night. Funnels can take some practice to locate on topographical maps. I was fortunate to be able to pour over maps with John for hours. We reviewed a half dozen lakes with John coaching me on the best funnels in each body of water. It's also important to remember not all funnels are created equal.

Generally speaking, the narrower the funnel the better. Additionally, the best funnels terminate in areas that contain structure and cover that create a feeding ground for big bass. John also emphasized that big bass are creatures of habit. They will move from their daytime bedrooms (offshore suspension) to their nighttime kitchens (shallow water feeding grounds) at a cadence you could use to set your watch.

As a last question about funnels, I asked John to explain exactly how he would go about fishing one. John said, "A big bass is like a bulldog. She suspends offshore during the day alone. At night she follows a funnel in and hunts alone. Big dogs don't eat out of the same bowl. This phenomenon means you're targeting a lone fish, and just like if you were deer hunting a dominant buck, you've got to seek them out at a choke point; hence the power of the funnel." John further recommended anchoring his boat a short cast from the narrowest portion of the funnel and saturation casting the area. "Intermittingly, I'll work plastic lures through the same area. It's tough to beat a black and blue jig." Interestingly, John's comment on a black and blue jig closely coincides with data mined in *High Percentage Fishing*.

> **Lunker Lore**: When I asked John about the best speed to move plastic bait at night his comment was, "You can't move them too slowly at night. I've been woken from a dead sleep before from a big bass hitting a lure that had not moved in who knows how long!"

Toledo Bend Funnel

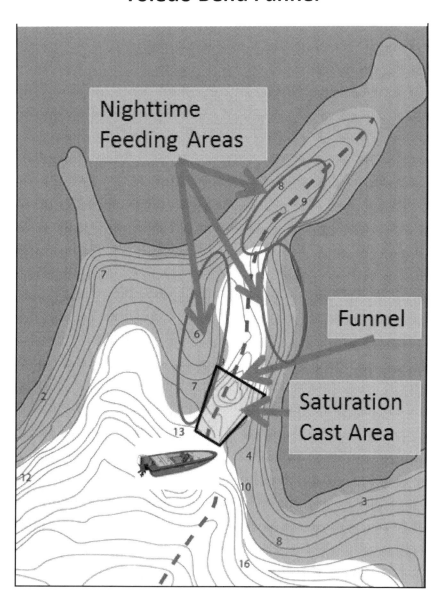

When to Fish

Some of the best night fishermen begin fishing for pre-spawn giants as early as January when water temperatures reach 50 degrees in the Deep South. At the beginning of the year there will be many slow outings and fishermen are well advised to carefully pick their nights on the water to maximize their chances. The first series of two or three days of southern winds and warm nights in the spring can get big females fired up and staging outside of spawning areas. Northern shores often are the best places to capitalize on this phenomenon as warm surface water will collect in this area of the lake. During cold water periods crawfish are often denned up and this will dictate the use of slower moving underwater baits such as a jig. Wood and rock are preferred cover. Water clarity is particularly important early in the year. Cold muddy water creates some of the most challenging fishing conditions an angler can encounter. If heavy rains muddy the water, it's best to stick to daylight hours. Nighttime bite windows during this time often peak shortly after sunset and slow considerably as the lake water gets colder as the night progresses. I rarely fish past 10 pm in the spring.

> **Lunker Lore:** Rock piles near the surface can absorb heat on sunny days and extend the night bite early in the year as they radiate heat into the night in surrounding water keeping it warmer longer.

Outside of the cold-water periods (water temps below 60 degrees,) big bass will feed on and off throughout most of the night. The best predictor of a bite window is when the fish last fed, but this information, is of course, impossible to know. The biggest fish will leave their daytime haunts and head shallow to feed at dusk. A secondary bite window often occurs two hours after sunset. Nighttime fishing is notorious for extended lull periods punctuated by aggressive feeding. Patience and perseverance rule the night. The last feeding window typically occurs just before sunrise.

> **Lunker Lore**: Weeds release oxygen during the day through the process of photosynthesis. At night this process reverses and oxygen is consumed. During the hottest parts of the year, when weed growth is at its maximum, heavily weeded bays can fish very poorly late into the night and into early morning as oxygen levels are at their lowest levels in any given 24-hour period. As the sun rises photosynthesis begins anew for the day. Oxygen levels are replenished and fish activity picks back up.

The Moon

If you ask a dozen different fishermen their opinion of which moon phase is the best to fish, you are likely to get a dozen different answers. Some anglers are fierce apologists for the increased light levels associated with full moons, while others much prefer the concealment of a new moon. Indeed, brighter nights linked to full moons make fishing easier, but easy doesn't necessarily mean better. There are no conclusive studies on this subject that answer this question definitively. The few studies that have been done, including the analysis of my own data, indicates that there is no increase in catch rates associated with particular moon phases. That said, there is some anecdotal evidence that new moons typically fish better for trophy class fish than full moons. Richie White, a popular guide and nighttime expert on Lake Fork, completed an examination of the top 50 bass caught in Texas and noted that none were caught during a full moon. Some of my favorite nights to fish are on new moons with overcast drizzly skies.

I believe that the best moon phases depend on the lake, the season, and more specifically the water clarity. I favor darker moon phases on warm or clear water and brighter phases on cold or stained waters. In any case, as compared to fishing during the day, virtually any night dramatically increases your chances at a lunker fish regardless of the moon phase. The chart on the next page summarizes the best nighttime bite windows by month.

Night Time Lures

Many fishermen overthink nighttime lure selection. The simple rule of thumb is that if it works during the day, the same lure will work at night. Beyond this guideline, I recommend imagining the moon as the sun and selecting lures the same way you would during the day based on light levels. My experience indicates that topwater lures and moving baits with lots of vibration fish better during lower light levels associated with a new moon, and more natural and subtle plastics such as worms and jigs fish

Peak Fishing Times by Month

Time	Jan	Feb	March	April	May	June	July	Aug	Sep	Oct	Nov	Dec
5pm												
6pm												
7pm												
8pm												
9pm												
10pm												
11pm												
12pm												
1am												
2am												
3am												
4am												
5am												
6am												
7am												

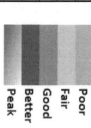

Peak
Better
Good
Fair
Poor

better during the brighter light levels associated with full moons. Of course, if you have cloudy skies, the moon phase is irrelevant, and you should fish the lake as though the moon was new.

All this said, the dominant big fish lure at night is a jig. Topwater lures may often catch more fish, but it's rare they will outproduce jigs in terms of size. In fact, I think one of the biggest mistakes trophy fishermen can make is getting caught up in the action produced by topwaters. If your goal is the biggest bass possible, more often than not you may be doing yourself a disservice fishing a topwater lure. After jigs, the next best nighttime big bass bait is a large 10" + plastic worm. These large baits move water and create a strong contrast making them easy for fish to locate at night.

Color

Hands down black is the best color for nighttime fishing. When fishing surface lures, black creates the greatest contrast with the lighter night sky. Some anglers prefer white lures for bottom bouncing baits as it creates more contrast with darker bottoms. However, my experience is that in all cases black baits out-produce any other color.

> **Lunker Lore:** In stained water, vibration and scent can dramatically increase catch rates. However, in the clearest waters, too much noise or vibration can deter fish.

Anchoring

A fundamental mistake made by many nighttime anglers is constantly moving and searching for fish. While this may be a good small fish strategy, it's a poor way to chase giants. The biggest bass in a system is also the wariest in a system. I highlighted a story in *High Percentage Fishing* that demonstrated just how sensitive big bass can be to boat noise, fish finders, and trolling motors. John Hope also told me that he had been studying a fish at night which had been feeding back and forth on a small stretch of shoreline for a couple of hours. At one point during the evening, a child ran out on the dock and immediately John was able to see with his radio tracker that the big fish had swum off. She completely left the area, and did not return to her regular pattern until well after the child left. One of the best ways to avoid spooking fish is to anchor your boat on a known big bass haunt. The best locations are funnel points, offshore humps, underwater lights, or feeding benches as described in the public water fishing section of this book.

> **Lunker Lore**: Once anchored it can take up to 15 minutes for the area to settle and for spooked fish to return to their regular feeding habits. Patience is a virtue of the nighttime trophy bass fisherman that cannot be overstated.

Underwater Lights

If you fish a lake that does not have underwater lights

it's possible to create your own. There are videos available on the internet on sites such as YouTube that outline how to create your own underwater light with LEDs. These lights are powered by DC voltage and can be powered off your boat's 12V batteries while anchored. Here again, patience is a necessary virtue. Once positioned, these lights can take several hours to set the food chain into motion and draw in larger predator fish. I've experimented with these lights in a limited fashion with moderate success. In the future, I plan to spend more time with the concept as I believe it could be a key tactic in improving big fish catch rates on bodies of water with few traditional structures to concentrate big fish.

Boat Lights

I debated at considerable length whether to include this paragraph in the book simply because of the safety implications. All states require navigational lights to be used on public water after dark. Failing to do so leads to boat collisions that result in dozens of fatalities annually. No fish is worth dying over and not using your lights is just as foolhardy as fishing in a lightning storm. All that said, I am convinced that big fish are spooked by most above water boat lights. The shallower you are the more negative this effect becomes. To whatever extent it's possible, anglers are well advised to minimize extra lighting in boats at night. Spotlights, rail lighting, large headlamps, all such devices dilate your eyes reducing nighttime vision while also spooking big fish.

> **Lunker Lore**: The spectrum of light created by black lights has very little ability to penetrate water and as such is not visible to fish more than a few feet deep. Black lights also have the added benefit that they light up fluorescent line making bite detection easier. Beyond navigational lights, if I'm using surface lights in my boat at night, black lights are preferred.

Noise

With your sense of sight severely reduced in low light conditions, your sense of hearing becomes exponentially more important. Bite detection on topwaters and general awareness of approaching hazards are all improved through the sense of hearing at night. Sounds made above the water, such as talking, don't spook bass as they are not readily transmitted to the water. However, noises made through the boat hull are tantamount to an underwater drum and they may well spook fish. Treat trophy hunting bass at night the same way you would hunting a trophy deer in a stand. Be as quiet and deliberate as possible.

Sneaking Baits

One of the best big fish presentation strategies I have discovered at night is fishing large baits, both on top of and below the surface, as stealthily as possible. This approach is a particularly useful tactic on calm quiet nights. A creature moving across a lake at night knows danger lurks below and it isn't likely to make a major commotion moving across the water. I believe big bass can quickly learn to associate negative experiences with noisy nighttime lures. There have been times where I could not catch a fish over 3lbs on a buzzbait, but when I put on a Jitter Bug and worked it as quietly as possible in the same area I caught multiple big fish.

Stitching

Stitching is a method developed and popularized by famed big bass fisherman Bill Murphy. The method is simple: work your soft plastics across the bottom as slowly as possible while keeping your fingers in constant contact with your line. The specifics of the method for holding the line come down to angler preference, but the key is constant contact. Many studies have shown that anglers miss a far larger percentage of strikes than most would ever care to know. Advances in rod and line technology have come a long way over the years in helping to increase bite detection, but there is still no better way than tactile contact with your line.

Insect Repellent

One of the biggest complaints anglers have about nighttime fishing is the dramatic increase of nuisance insects, such as mosquitoes, as soon as the sun goes down. The worst approach possible to deal with this winged irritation is to use spray on insect repellent. Bug spray is one of the best fish repellents out there! No matter how careful you are it's virtually impossible to apply the stuff without accidental contamination on your hands which will invariably wind up on your lure. If you are fishing moving baits you might be able to get away without a significant issue, but if you are fishing slow moving plastics your bite rate will suffer. Furthermore, many bug repellents can damage the screens on expensive electronics. They are best left out of the boat altogether. Fortunately, most flying insect activity dies down as the night progresses. Often the swarms at sunset have completely vanished a few hours after dark.

> **Lunker Lore**:   If chemical repellent truly is necessary, consider a device such as Thermacell which will provide a radius of protection without direct exposure to the angler.

Retrieves

During daylight hours, catch rates can often be increased through changes in the retrieve speed. Injecting a degree of erratic behavior in lures imitates wounded prey fish and triggers bites.   While I have caught bass at night on varied retrieves, I've found that my hook up percentages are far higher with steady retrieves, particularly with moving baits such as buzzbaits or spinnerbaits. While bass are proficient nocturnal feeders, they can and do miss moving baits. Injecting additional complexity to the matter by changing retrieval speeds makes a tough situation worse for the bass.

The primary exception to the rule above is pausing baits. Floating topwaters or plastics that can be stopped on the bottom are examples of lures that can see bite rates skyrocket through the use of periodic stops during the retrieve. Often a bass will trail behind a lure and never commit to hitting it before the retrieve is completed. This same bass, however, may violently strike the bait if stopped. With floating topwaters, I will often let a lure sit for a short period after splashdown. Bass in the area will be drawn to the noise and often strike the lure before it moves.

> **Lunker Lore:** The ideal length of a pause varies by the night and the overall aggression of the fish. Sometimes pauses of a few seconds are sufficient, other times, a pause of a minute or more may yield improved catch rates. If you've done much night fishing, you've undoubtedly made a cast and then had to deal with tangled line. Many anglers have been surprised by a giant hitting their stationary lure several minutes into working to untangle a bird's nest in their reel.

Topwater Lures

There is an adage in nighttime topwater fishing, "wait for the weight." One of the biggest mistakes fishermen make while night fishing topwater lures is setting the hook to the explosive sound of a topwater hit. Because bass feed less efficiently at night, they may not have fully engulfed the lure and setting the hook too early pulls it right out of their mouth. Anglers are well advised to continue their normal retrieve for a second or two after a strike, waiting until they feel the weight of the fish load on the rod before setting the hook. The key is to wait while not allowing slack to build in the line. This concept is much easier said than done and even seasoned anglers can fall victim to setting the hook too quickly.

Scents

During daylight fishing I do not believe supplementary scents increase catch rates sufficiently to justify their expense. Most plastics manufactured today come with a scent applied during the production process. Many studies have shown that while scents probably don't hurt catch rates, they probably don't help near as much as most might think. Their overall benefit comes down to an individual evaluation of the economics of the matter. I do believe scents can be powerful aids to nighttime anglers who are methodically saturation fishing a particular spot. The slow nature of the fishing allows the scent to build up in the area and can improve catch rates.

Line

When night fishing, always fish line significantly heavier than you do during the day. A fish's ability to see line at night is dramatically reduced, and catch rates don't suffer in the same way they do during the day with increased line size. There is no reason not to use heavier line at night. Laziness can be an angler's worst enemy resulting in lost trophies.

Shallow Water Fish

Shallow water fish can be spooked at night when

other fish are caught. If the bite dies after a hookup, but I know the shallow water spot holds fish, I'll often return about a half hour later and almost immediately hook up again. In much the same way as the milk run strategy for underwater lights, anglers can employ a similar strategy with smaller shallow water hot spots.

Lunker Lore: My experience has been that deeper water fish are not affected in the same way. One word of caution is that if you are fishing a deep school, day or night, if you significantly injure a fish it may be best to hold it in your live well until you are done with the spot. Studies conducted by Bob Underwood indicate that a hooked fish with a skin puncture outside the mouth, which results in bleeding, releases a stress hormone that can be detected by the other fish. In a school this hormone can effectively shut the bite down. A short time spent in a live well with rejuvenation salts is probably best for the injured fish whether you buy into this theory or not.

Tips, Tricks, and Nighttime Safety

• Safety Glasses

If I'm fishing topwater lures at night, particularly if there is a second angler in the boat, I'm wearing safety glasses. Setting a hook on a missed strike can result in a lure hurling back at the boat like a bullet. The risk of a hook in the eye isn't worth the small inconvenience of wearing safety glasses.

- Life Jacket

If you are out at night, wear one. There are countless versions on the market these days that can be worn in complete comfort. Many lakes become ghost towns at night. Help, if needed, may not be readily available. Here again, the risk of not wearing a jacket far outweighs the inconvenience. Sadly, more than one able-bodied angler has drowned at night after falling into cold water only to discover the water has sapped them of the necessary strength to pull themselves back into the boat.

- Launching

Launch close to where you are going to fish. Running at night, even if you know the lake, can be extremely dangerous. You never know when a widow-maker log has floated out into the boat lane after a storm. It's far safer to take the extra couple of minutes to trailer on down to the next boat launch.

- Running

As mentioned above running at night can be extremely dangerous. Floating items in the lake can be impossible to see; fish finders can create an intense light that even at nighttime settings can temporarily reduce nighttime vision. If you must run, make sure you go as slowly as possible to stay on plane. Running on lakes with many homes on them can be particularly dangerous as navigational lights on stationary boats can look virtually identical to a dock light on the other side of the lake. Every year people die in these sorts of tragedies where stationary boats are hit by well-meaning anglers who simply didn't see them. A corollary of this is that nighttime anglers are well advised to be wary of high traffic areas of lakes and avoid anchoring down near them. Even with your navigation lights on you could still be missed.

- Headlamps

Invest in a good headlamp with multiple lumination options. As previously mentioned, try to avoid using them as much as possible as I believe they spook big fish. However, they are indispensable when unhooking a fish or retying. They are also a great safety tool as an extra method to warn an approaching boat of your position.

- Weather

Check the weather before heading out for the night. More than once I've spent hours getting poured on while hiding out on shore during a thunderstorm that unexpectedly rolled up. Beating a storm back to the boat launch isn't always an option when you are on the other side of the lake and can't safely run back. High winds can also quickly turn calm waters into rough waters which might be virtually impossible to navigate at night when you cannot see the direction of the waves.

- Scouting

Scout fishing areas in the daylight. Mark hazards such

as stumps, trees, and floating buoys on your GPS. I never fish an area at night I have not previously fished in the daylight.

- Check Boat Lights

Boats are notorious for random, seemingly inexplicable electrical issues. Just because your lights worked the last trip doesn't mean they will this time. It could be a long, dangerous run back to the ramp if you realize the lights don't work when you power them on for the first time as the sun sets.

- Meticulous Organization

As a final tip, organization goes a long way at making night fishing more enjoyable. Sloppy housekeeping can make it hard to find lures or worse yet cost precious seconds when searching around for a pair of needle-nose pliers to remove a hook. Before you head out have a place for everything and everything in its place.

Section III

Private Water

Private Water Fishing

"After he has studied it for a lifetime it is not less mysterious but more so, more strange and so more alluring." - Odell Shepard

Mike Frazier with a Camelot Bell giant!

If you've ever flown over the continental U.S., you have no doubt noticed there are a remarkable number of ponds and small lakes that dot the countryside. The vast majority of these impoundments are run of the mill farm ponds that entertain small children and adults alike in the warmer months with consistent action on bluegills and the occasional bass. Indeed, many of us first got hooked on the sport of bass fishing while floating a nightcrawler on a farm pond under one of Grandpa's old bobbers.

Many of these ponds were impounded decades ago with the assistance of subsidies from the local, state, or federal governments who viewed ponds as strategically helpful. Others were created purely for leisure. Most of these backyard ponds are lightly managed, and frequently run into problems with numerous stunted fish making up a majority of the population. What few new pond owners realize is that properly maintaining a pond, particularly if the goal is the creation of a trophy class fishery, is incredibly time and resource demanding.

As we have previously shown, adding even 1lb of weight to a largemouth bass, requires approximately 1,000 shad. Purchased for a few dollars a dozen you'd be looking at $2,500 to grow a single bass to ten pounds. This, of course, assumes that you are trying to grow just that one fish. Ponds have lots of competition. To give you an idea of the full scope of the potential cost, I'm aware of a 90-acre lake in South Texas commissioned by a wealthy landowner and managed by a fish biologist. The biologist said, "In the spring they would stock the lake with 10,000 pounds of shiners, nearly half a million threadfin shad, 10,000 pounds of tilapia, and however much else could be scraped up in gizzard shad and bluegill." These stockings ran into the hundreds of thousands of dollars annually, and the bass population could decimate this forage base in a matter of weeks. More than one expert I spoke to said it was economically impossible for most small lake owners to stock their way into big bass.

Beyond the required forage base, there are a myriad of other issues that must be dealt with to create a true trophy class fishery. The process begins with the design of the lake. A common mistake made during the initial excavation is digging the lake too shallow and digging near flood-prone areas. Shallow lakes can quickly become weedy lakes, and weeds create hiding places for prey fish that ultimately reduce the feeding efficiency of bass. Deeper lakes also moderate temperatures, reducing heat stress in the summer and cold strain in the winter. Flood-prone lakes can run the risk of introducing inferior genetics from nearby bodies of water. Once dug, the next step in lake building is establishing a bountiful and self-sustaining forage base. While the specifics of the forage base have many regional considerations, most owners focus on bluegill and shad. Building a massive forage base can often take 2-3 years depending on the level of management. Introducing bass to the ecosystem before this point can have catastrophic results. Once the forage base is selected, bass fry with superior genetics need to be stocked. Debates rage over where the best genetics can be procured, but virtually all those serious about creating a trophy class lake select purebred Florida-strain largemouth. Naturally, the better the genetics, the more expensive the fry become. These fish have fast growth rates and top end size that can be nearly double that of northern-strain fish. The downside to these fish is that they are more susceptible to cold weather kills and are notoriously harder to fool into biting artificial lures than their northern-strain cousins.

From here owners must closely monitor the forage base, and water quality. Fish with the best genetics can attain remarkable size in relatively short periods. Year old fish that top the scales at three pounds are not impossible. After all this expense and effort, owners face perhaps their most difficult challenge: culling. Culling is the process of population control in a bass lake. Simply said, it's removing fish to keep the total number of mouths to feed low enough that the remaining fish can reach gargantuan sizes as rapidly as possible. Depending on the scale of the lake, thousands of fish may have to be removed annually for the remainder to have any real chance of trophy potential. There are two primary approaches to achieve this, both of which have tradeoffs. The first is traditional angling and removing all fish caught below a certain size. The major downside to this method is that it takes a lot of fishing to remove enough bass to make a difference and this process can quickly leave behind a population of educated lure shy bass. The second is the use of shock boats, which emit an electric shock into the water which temporarily stuns fish allowing the smaller fish to be scooped up in nets and removed. Shock boats are expensive to operate, and they also miss a significant portion of fish as they have limited ranges. Compounding matters, traditional fishing often suffers for weeks after a lake is shocked.

While expensive and daunting, several people across the country live and breathe private water bass fishing at a level few can comprehend. These big bass dreamers and innovators may well have the best chance of anyone in the world at growing and catching a bass that beats the North American World Record of 22lbs 4 oz., held by George Perry since 1932. Later in this section, we will look at two such individuals and their lakes, La Perla and Camelot Bell. The owners of these lakes have poured their heart, soul, and personal wealth into a vision many call foolhardy; the creation of the perfect largemouth bass lake.

Ethics of Private Water Fishing

Some view fishing private waters as "high fence fishing." In the world of hunting, high fence refers to a practice where animals are hunted on highly managed fenced tracts of land. In some states, this can amount to little more than wealthy individuals showing up and taking an animal at a considerable distance with a rifle while it partakes in its predictable daily routine which invariably includes a stop at a feeder. I've always been less than impressed with these "trophy hunts" and have long considered meat and mounts taken from high fenced hunts as a small step above shopping at the grocery store. So how similar is trophy fishing on private water to high fence hunting? In my pursuit of locating the ideal water, I sat down with some of the best big bass sticks in the country to get their perspective. The theme that emerged was that private water fishing was wholly different from any form of high fenced hunting.

First, by that definition, virtually all freshwater fishing could be considered high fence, as all lakes are bound by their shorelines. Bass are not free to come and go from lake to lake. Some lakes are vastly larger than others, but there are plenty of lakes in California, for instance, that are quite small and have produced a majority of the fish that comprise the top 25 biggest largemouths ever caught. Lake Dixon, which produced Dottie, the heaviest largemouth ever weighed at 25.1lbs, is a mere 70 acres and was regularly stocked by the state of California with trout. These fish were then voraciously fed upon by the largemouth in the lake. If the size of the lake is all that mattered, one could build a compelling case that a 13lb fish out of the sizable Lake Fork is a greater accomplishment than a 20lb fish out of tiny Dixon.

For fun, let's carry the hunting argument out a bit further. Consider for a moment a hypothetical 500-acre hunting plot. Well managed land can support roughly one deer for every ten acres. Therefore, a 500-acre plot could hold up to 50 deer. I think few folks would take an ethical issue with an individual stalking deer on a 500-acre plot with a bow. If we consider the space a deer occupies, roughly two feet wide by four feet long, we could say an average deer occupies eight square feet. 500 acres amounts to around 22 million square feet. If we then divide this sum by the space occupied by the 50 deer we would see that we are searching for creatures occupying one unit of space for every 100,000 units of available space. Let's now run this same math for a hypothetical 50-acre bass lake averaging eight feet in depth. A well-managed lake can carry as many as two trophy fish per acre. Since bass can move through the water three-dimensionally, we need to find the cubic area available for movement. Running this math yields roughly 18 million square feet of open space to occupy. If we then divide this by the area a trophy fish takes up, we arrive at a search area of 180,000 units for every one unit occupied by a trophy fish. Through this comparison, we can show that from a strictly mathematical point of view, it would be at least twice as hard to locate a trophy bass on a 50-acre body of water than to find a deer on a 500-acre tract of land.

    Math aside, there are countless other factors that make contacting a trophy fish far more complicated than finding a deer. For starters, you can see deer. In most bodies of water, you cannot see more than a few feet, and thus 99% of the area of the lake is invisible to you at any given time. Beyond this, deer only move in one plane, while bass can move three-dimensionally through their environment. Furthermore, once located, a deer cannot choose whether or not to eat a bullet fired from your gun. A bass, on the other hand, assuming you are lucky enough to put a lure in front of her, will in all probability choose not to eat your bait. Studies conducted by Doug Hanson, the bass professor, have shown that the average consumption rate of an artificial lure, when presented to a wild bass, is roughly 10%.

Some folks may never be comfortable with the thought of highly managed fisheries. There is no doubt that catching a trophy fish on a large public body of water is a harder task than catching one on private water. I make no argument to the contrary. Furthermore, I do believe there should be separate records kept for private and public water fish. However, to assume that fishing private water is tantamount to hunting a high fenced property underestimates many of the fundamental differences in the two pursuits.

Others will complain about the high costs often associated with gaining access to private waters. Indeed, it can be expensive, but the reality is the vast majority of these waters are within reach of the regular working-class man if he so desires to align his priorities accordingly. In fact I'm aware of several trophy bass fishermen, who view private water fishing as being cheaper than what most weekend bass anglers spend on an annual basis. These folks rarely own boats, considering them expensive to purchase and maintain. They also want to maximize their odds with the limited time they have available to fish. Indeed, when you add up boat payments, maintenance costs, fuel, launch fees; it's easy to see how your average weekend angler could easily afford many annual trips to even the most expensive private water fisheries. Sure, if that same fisherman owned a boat he could fish more often, but fishing more often, particularly if it's in poor water, may never translate into a giant bass.

Through my research and personal experience, I've come to believe that at the right time, with the proper knowledge, your odds of catching a trophy fish can be as high as 50% in a single day on some of the best private waters in the world. To be sure, there is no such thing as a guarantee. Chris Mahfouz of Houston, Texas is one of the best big bass fishermen in the state. To his name, Chris has more than 150 fish he's boated that top the scales over 10 pounds. He's caught scores of giants on both private and public water. In one discussion I had with Chris on Camelot Bell, he told me he had fished the lake dozens of times, catching many double-digit fish up to 15lbs, but he also confessed he had been skunked on the lake more times than he cared to remember.

Ultimately, anglers in search of the fish of a lifetime have a decision to make. An ideological decision to exclude private water fishing may limit their top end trophy potential and exclude them from a wide swath of bass fishing which can be highly rewarding. In the end, I believe private and public pursuits of trophy fish are not mutually exclusive. If you want to maximize your odds, have the broadest experiences, and cross paths with some of the biggest bass out there; hit them both and hit them hard.

La Perla

"The true angler can welcome even a low river and a dry year, and learn from it, and be the better for it, in mind and in spirit." - G.M.W. Wemyss

Aerial image of La Perla

In a dusty southwest corner of Texas, not far from the Mexican border, sits La Perla Ranch. In the early 2000s Dr. Gary Schwarz purchased the 15,000-acre ranch to subdivide into smaller 1,250-2,500 tracts which he could improve and then flip for a profit. Gary, a highly regarded oral surgeon, has had a keen interest in hunting and fishing since his youth. He gained notoriety in the hunting world in the 1980s when he invented a multi-step food plot process that created enormous growth in whitetail deer. Historically in arid regions the size of deer ran small because the agricultural and native food base did not provide adequate nutrition to grow world-class animals. In a matter of a few years, Gary's food plot innovations began producing massive deer in the tumbleweeds of South Texas which rivaled the biggest deer harvested anywhere in the country. From this success Gary founded Tecomate Seed Company which evolved over the years to include the buying and selling of ranches.

This story, of course, does not end with big deer. In May of 2016, I had the great fortune to speak with Dr. Schwarz at length about a project he had been working on for more than a decade that may ultimately culminate in the creation of one of the best bass lakes in the world. In 2004, while subdividing La Perla, Gary decided he would keep a 1,700-acre parcel for himself. This section contained a mud hole of a lake that sparked his imagination one day while he was operating a bulldozer to improve the land. As an avid fisherman, he wondered what it would take to improve the small nearly lifeless lake into something he could enjoy recreationally. In the coming weeks, Gary spent endless hours poring over everything he could soak up on the web. In doing so, he stumbled across a publication called *Pond Boss*. Gary phoned the company and ordered a copy of every magazine and book they had ever published. The owner of the company was stunned by Gary's desire to learn. He flew down shortly after and met with him offering specific advice on creating a world-class private lake. To round out his education, soon after Gary hired renowned fisheries biologist John Jones. From there he purchased his own heavy equipment and began to expand the size of the existing lake drastically. In the coming months, under John's guidance, La Perla Lake began to take shape from the clay-laden ground.

When completed, the lake was 88 acres with dozens of islands, points, and bays extending the fishable water and shoreline habitat to more than 7 miles. The maximum depth of the lake is 22 feet. To keep

Dr. Gary Schwarz with a La Perla giant

weed growth propagation low there is very little shallow water, and most of the lake exceeds 8 feet. To combat stratification and the high heat of south Texas, Gary also added miles of aeration tubes which dramatically increased the biomass carrying capacity of the lake. Initially, bluegill, shad, and shiners were introduced to the lake as forage fish. They were then allowed to propagate predator-free for a period to establish a sustainable population. Dozens of pellet feeders were added around the lake to maximize growth and reproduction of the forage fish. Then, with John's guidance, Gary selected high growth pure Florida-strain largemouth bass to stock in the lake. As the fish quickly grew, their voracious appetites decimated the baitfish population and Gary began to research various options to replenish their numbers. After running the math, he realized ongoing stocking of forage fish would quickly become cost prohibitive. It was at this time, around 2007, that Gary's private lake education and trophy deer background collided leading to a series of innovations that may well leave ripples for decades across the world of trophy bass fishing.

Gary built a series of small feeder ponds at a raised elevation above La Perla. The concept, while not a new one in and of itself, was to grow forage fish in a predator-free environment until they reached an ideal size at which point they could be released into the lake through a large drain. While the process worked, the effort was not translating into the growth Gary had hoped to see. In 2008 his fish were undersized for their age. In an attempt to solve the problem Gary began to research a variety of forage options and finally stumbled across freshwater prawns. These creatures, essentially a type of shrimp, have elongated pincers that can bring their total length up to nearly two feet when fully grown. They also happen to be easy to raise and, as Gary soon discovered, far more efficient than forage fish at turning feeder pond nutrients into protein bass can eat. Prawns are aggressive eaters, and while maturing in the forage ponds, they are king of their domain knowing no predators. As such, once released into La Perla, they are fearless, making them easy prey for bass to consume. While the concept may be unsettling to some, the results Gary experienced in increased growth rates in his bass were nothing short of miraculous. In a single year the bass went from being undersized to more than 10% over their expected weight. Three years later the lake produced its first 10lb fish.

While his prawns were rapidly growing his bass, Gary was becoming increasingly frustrated with how difficult his fish were to catch. Florida-strain bass are notoriously weather sensitive and far harder to fool with traditional angling methods than their northern-strain counterparts. Gary began seeking advice from well-known anglers on how to combat this and was swayed to introduce Florida and northern-strain crossbred bass known as F1 integrates into the system. Unknown at the time to Dr. Schwarz, this would become his biggest mistake. As he would later discover, northern-strain genetics are dominant and over successive generations eventually displace the top end growth potential of Florida-strain genes. Once released, this genie was impossible to put back in the bottle. Devastated by his mistake, Gary began exploring his options and soon resolved to learn from his mistake and keep moving forward by building a second lake.

Rising from the ashes of La Perla, Jalisco Lake was soon born on the ranch. At full pool the lake is nearly 60 acres in size and attempts to right the mistakes made in Gary's first lake in every possible way. Brilliantly designed, the lake has four forage ponds, which when combined total thirty acres or nearly 50% the total capacity of Jalisco. As a comparison, La Perla's feeder ponds only totaled 12 acres or roughly 13% of its size. Jalisco also has extensive shallow water areas which Gary hopes will make fishing easier. In the center of the lake, there is raised rectangular wetland. Beautifully symbiotic, the marsh attracts ducks in the fall for hunting and provides pristine habitat for crawfish. The crawfish reproduce at astounding rates and naturally propagate into the lake creating fantastic forage for bass. Much like La Perla, Jalisco was also stocked with feeder fish which were allowed to reproduce extensively before largemouth bass were added.

Gary has also greatly improved his process for growing prawn in feeder ponds. He learned during his experiments at La Perla that in early years it was easy to drain the shallow feeder ponds and all its content into the main body of water. However, as the years progressed the ponds began to fill with weeds which the prawn would hang onto. This decreased his transfer rates by as much as 15%. To combat this, he discovered goldfish stocked with the prawn at precise levels consumed the weeds, eliminating this problem and in doing so attained perfect forage size themselves. Further improving this process, Gary also discovered that adding threadfin shad several months after the prawn had been introduced increased the biomass produced in the feeder pond even more. The shad are prolific multipliers and consume different food bits than the prawn. The prawn eat some of the shad and as a result grow up to 30% larger. Gary's feeder pond rotation now includes his unique blend of prawn, goldfish, and shad with the occasional pond being dedicated to bluegill production to supplement the main lake population.

Perhaps most exciting and controversial of all is the origin of the particular genetic strain of bass Dr. Schwarz released into his new lake. Years in the making, in 2014 Gary entered into a legally binding contract with the Texas Parks and Wildlife Division. (TPWD) In this agreement, Gary agreed to pay for all the ongoing expenses associated with Jalisco and to transfer all access rights to his new lake to TPWD for 15 years. In exchange, TPWD agreed to stock the lake with largemouth bass fry produced through its famed ShareLunker program. The Texas ShareLunker program is a statewide effort between TPWD and anglers to grow a world record largemouth bass. Any bass over 13lbs caught by an angler between October and May can be donated to the program in exchange for a replica of the fish. The program then seeks to breed these fish with large males creating offspring with superior genetics. In the case of the Jalisco fry, the mother was a 100% full Florida-strain bass bred with a male whose mother was a different 13lb 100% Florida-strain bass. The hope is that these superior genetics, which are expressed on both the paternal and maternal side of its lineage, will combine to create offspring with enormous top-end size potential.

The TPWD decision to stock a private lake with fry produced by the state-funded ShareLunker program was viewed as highly controversial by some. A few newspaper columnists in the state bashed the move as politically motivated and ethically untenable. Ideologically this viewpoint perhaps holds water, but it is ultimately deemed shortsighted by most who become educated on the specifics. Dr. Schwarz has made public his contract with the TPWD. Upon review, most rational minded readers can't help but conclude he got the short end of the stick in the deal. In essence, Gary handed over full access control of his lake to the state. The TPWD can drop by at any time to conduct research and no one, not even Dr. Schwarz, can fish the lake without their expressed approval. Jalisco has become a long-term experiment for which Gary bears the costs. His only reward over the next 15 years will simply be to see what's possible in the world of giant largemouth bass. Gary will be aged into his 80s by the time he gains back control of his lake. His price paid is hefty by all accounts, but Gary has weighed *knowing* worth it.

Recently La Perla has suffered from high salinity which likely stalled growth rates for the better part of two years.

To solve the problem Gary pumped nearly a billion gallons of water out of the lake and then prayed for rain. His prayers were answered in the fall with a series of torrential rains which returned the lake to full pool. Gary uses shock boats to cull fish. In 2016 he removed more than 7,000 bass from La Perla. In 2017 more than a thousand more fish were removed and transported to nearby Falcon Lake. Stocking fish of this size and genetic caliber on a public body of water is a fisherman's dream. The heavy culling has been paying off, and the remaining fish have swelled in size. A bass weighing 15.3lbs was shocked up in December of 2016. Gary may be disappointed with this F1 hybrid addition, but those genes will take a long time to proliferate, and even then, the lake will still have tremendous potential. La Perla undoubtedly has a bright future, but the twinkle in the good doctor's eye is Jalisco. The fish in that lake turned three in May of 2017 and the TPWD has already caught a fish that topped 7lbs. By May of 2018, the first double-digit bass will be prowling her waters.

For 13 years Dr. Schwarz has moved millions of cubic yards of dirt to make lakes. Along the way, he's innovated at every stage and pushed the boundaries of what's possible with largemouth bass. In the end, what Gary's after doesn't have fins; it's a desire to know. I strongly suspect he won't have to wait long to get his answers.

Camelot Bell

"Fishing is not an escape from life, but often a deeper immersion into it." -Harry Middleton

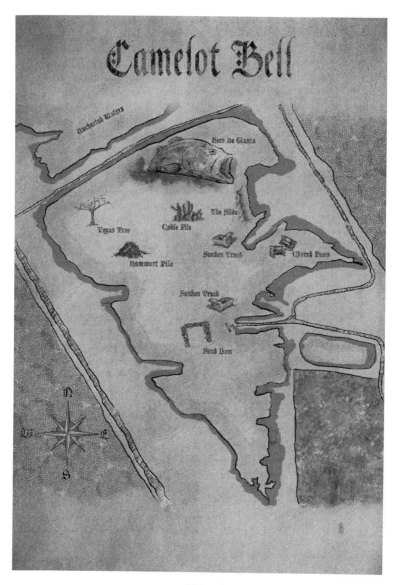

Perhaps one of the best known private water bass fisheries in the world is Camelot Bell in Coolidge, Texas. Its creator, Mike Frazier, whimsically named the lake after the castle and court associated with King Arthur and the Bell Sisters who previously owned the property. Mike impounded the lake in the late 1990s and it has been producing fish of increasingly impressive size ever since. The current lake record stands just north of 16lbs, and a double-digit fish out of this lake scarcely turns a head these days.

Early in the process of designing and building the lake, Mr. Frazier spared no expense attempting to create the best bass lake possible. Consulting with biologists and big bass experts from across the country, Mike pushed the envelope in terms of understanding big bass and their preferred environments. At full pool, Camelot Bell is roughly 50 acres, only slightly smaller than Lake Dixon, home to the famed Dottie who was chased relentlessly for years by California fishermen pursuing the world record. Speaking of world records, Mike is confident it is possible to match a fish of Dottie's caliber in private water, and he believes the recipe for doing so is simple: combine the best genetics with a never-ending smorgasbord of forage. After taking a year to establish a large base population of coppernose bluegill and threadfin shad in the lake Mike brought in 250 of the best strain of big bass genetics that could be found directly from Florida. His particular strain is known for a small grouping of effervescent blue scales which appears on the head of some fish, and for their incredible girth that extends well into the tail. Many other Florida genetics produce fish which have guts that abruptly end after the pectoral vent, which reduces their ability to carry weight across their full length. Simply put, Mike's fish weigh more per linear inch than just about any other bass on the planet. It took 5 years for Mike to grow and catch his first 10lb fish out of Camelot Bell. Since then he has allowed customers to fish the lake for a daily fee, and on an annual basis the lake arguably produces more ten-pound bass per acre than any other lake in existence. This achievement does not come easily or without enormous costs to Mike.

Dr. Joe Lambert with a Camelot Bell fish compared to the body type of many other Florida-strain bass

The lake is regularly fertilized with a proprietary elixir concocted by Mike to keep forage fish populations naturally reproducing in the lake at breakneck speeds. This high fertility translates into an enormous biomass that ultimately culminates in big bass, but it does come at the cost of reduced visibility. Water clarity on Camelot Bell is typically 1-2 feet, making sight fishing difficult to impossible. The lake contains no predator fish to compete with the largemouth for forage. No crappie, no catfish, no rough fish whatsoever beyond a few sterile grass carp placed in the lake to keep weed levels as low as possible. The lake was specifically designed and is actively managed to keep weed levels low. Mike believes plants create hiding places for bait fish which reduces the feeding efficiency of bass. In order to grow big fish, Mike wants his giants ponied up to the buffet line without any impediments. In regards to culling, Mike has all fish below 7lbs that are caught by anglers removed from the lake; no exceptions. As days progress, anglers fill their live wells and periodically drop fish off in a submerged fish trap located on the lake. Mike sells some of these fish for their genetic potential; others are transplanted to nearby lakes, or summarily consumed for the night's dinner. Tilapia are stocked in the fall as supplemental forage, and more recently Mike has been adding thousands of trout in the winter when water temperatures drop low enough to allow for their survival. If any trout made it through the winter they would die from the warm water in the Texas summer; however, few survive the big bass in the lake long enough to worry about such tribulations. As a final degree of asset protection, Camelot Bell is built on elevated acreage which effectively isolates it from genetic contaminants from any nearby bodies of water in the event of flooding. Front to back, Camelot Bell is designed, built, and maintained to be a one of a kind big bass producing machine.

Camelot Bell first came to my attention in early 2016 when chatter picked up about a series of 14lb+ fish the lake had recently produced. One of the first descriptions I heard of the lake came from a Texas Fishing Forum post by Ken Addington. With Ken's permission, I've reprinted the post with a few edits for clarity:

> Camelot Bell is a freak show for big bass. No doubt about it. Is it worth the money for two guys to fish all day? Maybe for some - others maybe not. It's all about your priorities. I landed a 15.0 there on Jan 7, 2012, and it was the lake record for about a month!
>
> For Rick Shipley and I on Feb 17th, it was PRICELESS! Rick has fished Fork and numerous other big bass factories with guides all over this great state and had not landed a legit DD in almost 40 years of bassin.
>
> We shoved off the dock at 8:00 am that morning and at 8:08 am I was netting his first fish of the day, a beautiful 11.5 pounder caught on a lizard. What a start! A while later I landed a 9.5 on a big crankbait, and two fish about the same size came unbuttoned in back to back casts.

We took a short break for lunch and hit it again about 1:00 pm. Right after lunch, the big girls started feeding, and Rick gets a 9.5 on a lizard near the dock. We moved across the lake near a little point, and Rick sticks a 10.5!! A few minutes later I catch a 12.0 on a lizard! Ten minutes after we get the 12 in the boat Ricks sets the hook on a MONSTER!! This fish comes up and wallows all over the place, and he finally works her to the boat. I slide the net under her, and she goes an even 13.0.

We now have a 10.5, a 12.0, and a 13.0 in the livewell. This all happened in about 30 minutes in a small area. I call Mike Frazier the owner and tell him about our catch, and he heads down to the dock with a big ice chest on a four-wheeler. As we are heading over to the dock, Rick sets the hook on another fish in the same area where his 13 just came from.

I grab the net and ask, "Is it another BIGGUN??!" The fish comes up and jumps, and Rick says, "Naww, it's just a little bitty one." He gets the fish to the boat and lips it. The fish pulls the Boga Grip to seven pounds.

I ask Rick when he decided that a SEVEN POUND fish was a "Little Bitty One" and we all laugh!! This lake will absolutely change your perception on what you think a big fish really is.

So at the end of the day, I asked Rick if it was worth the money he paid to fish. His response was, how do you put a price on a day of a lifetime?

Not to mislead you guys about the fishery. It is not a place where you catch a 100 bass a day. We had ten fish all day,

> but the top five went 56.5 pounds and was the lake record for best five until Justin Furnace from Cypress Texas hit the lake last week.
>
> All I can tell you is that it was nothing short of INCREDIBLE!!

Hot on my pursuit of my first double-digit bass I decided I had to fish the lake. Justin Furnace, of the nuclear day fame, had become one of my big bass mentors and had an upcoming trip planned to Bell which he agreed to let me join. In the weeks prior to the trip Justin educated me on big bass gear, tactics, and the fine nuances of the giants that swim the depths of Bell. From Justin's coaching, I learned Mike was incredibly protective of his big fish. Barbs on crankbaits were not allowed. Carolina rigs were banned, and any line lighter than 50lb braid was strongly frowned upon. Upon questioning about the line requirement Justin relayed to me a story from Dr. Joe Lambert (Doc), who has over a dozen fish to his name over 13lbs from both private and public water.

Doc was fishing Bell in spring searching for a true giant. He'd located a bed and caught a male off of it just shy of 8lbs. The water had been so murky he'd only got a glimpse of the female, but her tail appeared the size of a dinner plate. He made repeated casts to the approximate location of the bed and on the tenth or so cast she bit. The hook set felt like it went into a wall. Then the fish moved like a torpedo and pulled him down to his knees slamming his extra heavy rod onto the motor cowling snapping his 25lb fluorocarbon line before he ever got a chance to get his thumb on the release. She then jumped completely out of the water with his bait still in her mouth. Doc, no stranger to big fish, pegged her as a mid to upper teener. From then on, he's used 50-60lb braid almost exclusively when fishing the lake.

Justin advised, "I recommend braid, and if you do use fluorocarbon, use the heaviest stuff you can find, and make sure you use a Palomar knot. Your hooks need to be the strongest bass hooks you can find. Size 7 works well, but the real key is finding them made with extra thick wire. Anything less and the hooks will get straightened out. These fish are not normal bass; they are freaks of nature."

The Lake of Legends

Justin and I arrived at Camelot Bell late in the evening on a Tuesday in April of 2016. Mike Frazier has a beautiful cabin he allows guests to overnight in before their big day on the water. To add more gusto to the fevered hopes of first-time Camelot Bell fishermen, the cabin is dotted with mementos of huge fish caught over the years including the replica of an enormous fish I dare not guess the size of. Chomping at the bit for a little bass action, Justin and I attempted to night fish upon our arrival, but with a wild south wind blowing the task proved difficult. We quickly acquiesced to the sensibility of a good night's sleep before the marathon day of fishing we knew would follow.

Throughout the night an enormous thunderstorm raged. Like a child anticipating Christmas, I tossed and turned. Visions of giants danced in my head; yet between thunderclaps, part of me was concerned how the storm might impact the fishing. Somewhere in the early hours of the morning, I drifted off to sleep. We were awakened before sunup by an antsy call from Mike, wondering if we were ready to hit the water.

Justin and I did a final bit of preparation on our gear and headed down to the lake where we found Mike waiting for us. Within seconds of meeting Mike, I could tell he was different. With unbridled excitement he began to educate us about his lake and the beasts which lurked beneath its surface. He excitedly pointed out a nearby fish moving in the reeds. He coached us on the weather, he shared his recent observations of the lake, and he helped us craft a game plan for the day. Throughout it all, I had the sense we were just barely scratching the surface of a vast reservoir of bass knowledge. To say he is eccentric would be an understatement. Camelot Bell is his factory, and Mike Frazier is the Willy Wonka of bass fishing.

Out of a well-reasoned fear of the introduction of invasive species, with few exceptions Mike only allows fishermen to use a boat he provides. In sharp contrast to almost everything else about Camelot Bell, where no expense has been spared, the boat is aged with haggard carpet and a fiberglass gel coat which looks rough and worn. The boat has new seats, a functioning trolling motor and live well, but very little else. In reflection, despite its appearance, I cannot shake the thought that this one boat has likely born witness to the landing of more giant largemouth than perhaps any other that has ever existed. I never asked the question, but I suspect this is the very reason why Mike has not replaced it.

The water at Camelot Bell is stained. Visibility varies, but on this day, it did not exceed two feet. Virtually the entire lake is surrounded by a dense wall of reeds. With the lake being several feet high given unusual amounts of rainfall over the previous year, the water at the edge of the reeds varied from 5-8 feet deep. This trip was in late April, and Justin and I were hoping there might be a few laggard giants still spawning in the shallows.

We began by casting the reeds close to where we had launched the boat. Justin told me every inch of the lake held lunker potential, but that certain stretches of water were what he called, "nitro zones." These were areas that seemed to concentrate big fish. Our first couple of casts were uneventful. The shoreline reeds were so dense they almost resembled bamboo forests in some distant tropical land. Early on, I attempted to land my soft plastics as close to their edge as possible. As the day progressed, I abandoned this strategy and began bouncing my lure off the reeds and dropping it at their base. A few minutes into the trip, Justin pointed toward a small point and said, "Look, do you see that bass?" With a quick glance, I saw a huge dorsal fin and an even larger tail fin

Mike Frazier with a Camelot Bell DD

A view of Camelot Bell

sticking out of the water. I was stunned at the sheer enormity of the fish. I had to ask Justin, "Are you sure that's a bass?" In his usual southern drawl, Justin replied without hesitation, "Yesss'er, she's a giant." In turn, as stealthily as we could, Justin and I each landed our baits within a few feet of the fish, but we watched her slide off into the abyss, uninterested in our offers.

We continued around the lake and soon began catching fish. The first fish was a 2.5lb bass with the gut of a sumo wrestler. As I removed the fish, Justin pointed out one of the genetic distinctions of Camelot Bell bass: the frequent presence of an effervescent blue coloration on the scales near the top of the head and between the eyes. The fish was stunningly beautiful. I was about to release it back into the lake when Justin quickly reminded me of Mike's culling rule. Every fish under 7lbs gets removed. Justin told me we'd keep the fish in the livewell and when it got full, we would deposit them in a fish cage Mike kept on the lake.

The fishing continued this way for several hours. We were regularly catching fish, but the size rarely exceeded three pounds. Justin encouraged me repeatedly that morning saying, "The thing about Bell is that you're fishing for that one fish, that one bite. You are only ever one cast away." As the morning wore on, my mind occasionally drifted to other information I had learned about the lake. Ken Addington had spent hours educating me on the oddities of Camelot Bell over phone and e-mail. Camelot

Bell, Ken had said, "Is just different." Most lakes have peak bite windows around low-light periods. Not at Bell. The peak bite there seemed to be between noon and 3pm. The speculation was that given the low fishing pressure and the sheer quantity of forage in the lake, the fish ate when they wanted which typically aligned with the warmest part of the day. The lake also had a notoriously tough topwater bite. Drawn by the appeal of giant bass exploding on a surface bait, more than one angler has been skunked for extended periods on the lake throwing topwaters. Similarly, a few fishermen have attempted to fish at night with limited success. The fish just seem to prefer feeding midday. As Ken's words bounced around in my head, I was encouraged as we were rapidly approaching noon. Soon after the start of the witching hour, Justin boated a fat 8lber. A giant for most anglers Justin gave her little pause throwing her back saying, "There's fish in here more than twice that size!"

    Things stayed the same for the next couple of hours. We caught fish, but nothing of notable size. Around 3pm something happened, a window opened, it was like a switch had been flipped. The water began to buzz with life. Justin said, "Here's our shot, this is what we've been waiting for." Baitfish broke the surface all around us. Justin caught a solid 6lber. I cast my lizard into what appeared to be open water, perhaps 30 feet or so from the edge of a small patch of reeds that rose like a volcanic island from the deeper water that surrounded it. This area, known as *the slide*, was one of Justin's "nitro zones."

I can't be certain how deep the water was where my cast landed, but I suspected it to be eight feet or so. I counted down my lure for a handful of seconds until I was reasonably sure it rested on the bottom. When I raised my rod to lift the lure, I felt an unnatural weight that registers in all fishermen's brains as something other than a usual hang up. At that moment, decades of muscle memory from thousands of fish before served me well. I struck home a mighty hookset that pinged my line like a baseball off the sweet spot of a bat. I knew immediately I had hooked an enormous fish. My rod bowed up under her weight. For an instant the fish and the rod were locked in a titanic battle of inertia, neither willing to submit to the other. Then realizing she was hooked, the finned giant made a run for the surface with one powerful stroke of its tail. While maintaining pressure, I lowered my rod in a valiant attempt to keep the fish from breaching. She flashed near the surface, revealing herself for the first time, and I shouted to Justin, "She's a giant, big fish, grab the net, big fish!" Then, as quickly as she had come up, she plowed off to deeper water as though the hook, line, and steady punishment of the rod were little more than a nuisance to her afternoon feeding routine. In a few more seconds, my rod reached the end of its hyperbolic bend. The fish zinged drag as she drew out line. Having fought this battle in my mind countless times before, I was determined to better the beast as quickly as possible. The chance of some great misfortune, grew exponentially with the passage of each moment. I strained my equipment to the brink of failure and turned the fish from her deep water run. When she gave an inch, I took a mile, and reeled madly bringing her in hot as a fighter jet. In the background I could hear Justin scrambling for the net. He shouted, "Play her out, she's still too green; we will never get her in the net!" At that moment the fish made a heavy, powerful run straight beneath the boat. I followed her with my rod tip plunging it into the water. All the while my buckled down drag sang once again under the strain. Then she turned again and made a savage break for the surface emerging wild, gill plates wide, mouth open like a cavernous abyss. With a mighty head shake that threw water for yards. Justin shouted, "My God, she'll go 11, maybe more!" My hook held, and the fish submerged again, diminished now; a defeated green gladiator spent on the arena of Camelot Bell. She made one last futile effort to run but was turned again, this time into the net that awaited her. Justin and I both hooted at the top of our lungs. He celebrated this fish as if she were his own. Catching my first double-digit fish was a magic moment that had been decades in the making. It'll forever be engrained in my mind.

The Wolf Pack

The fish was enormous but it was clear she was spawned out. She bumped the scale at 26.5 inches with an 18" girth and weighed 10.5lbs. We quickly got her in the live well and took a minute to catch our breath and soak the moment in.

Author with a 10.5lb bass from Camelot Bell

We called Mike, and he came down to the dock to meet us. I got pictures with my trophy, and then Mike loaded the fish into a cooler full of water on the back of an ATV. My fish was destined to be part of the Wolf Pack.

Mike had built a new lake immediately adjacent to Camelot Bell he called the Wolf Pack Lake. For two full years, he had been stocking and breeding forage fish in the lake free of predators. This year, he was moving every double-digit fish caught out of Camelot Bell into the new lake. Where my fish fell, I can't recall, but by the end of the year, he had relocated over 75 double digit bass to the new lake. The largest was the lake record which topped 16lbs. Mike's intent was to allow these few fish to grow to gigantic proportions by gorging themselves over the winter on the abundant forage fish. A few large males had also been introduced. Mike expected in the spring these fish would spawn and create a lake full of genetic supertankers. They've done just that. In less than a year after the first spawn in the spring of 2017, the lake was filled with fish that topped the scales at more than 3lbs! In three to four more years, the lake will be full of double-digit fish born in the lake. The 75 supergiants originally stocked in the lake could potentially be gaining 2-4lbs annually. Running the math, the Texas State Record may already be swimming in the Wolf Pack Lake!

I once asked Mike how many double-digit fish he thought were in Camelot Bell. His reply was, "Hundreds, but the real question is how big is the largest fish in the lake?" This topic is one that is fiercely debated amongst those who have been lucky enough to have wet a line at Camelot Bell. Virtually everyone who has fished the lake has had an encounter with fish that seem to flirt with the supernatural. Justin told me, "There are absolutely 18+ pound fish in Camelot Bell. I have personally gotten very good looks at four separate fish on that lake that are in another league from the 15.5lber I caught." Others, including extremely respected big bass anglers who have handled more than their fair share of giant bass, claim there is without a doubt a world record swimming around

Wolf Pack Lake under construction

Wolf Pack Lake at full pool

in Bell. I've asked Mike his thoughts, and he humbly dances around the subject, but I know he believes she's there. The tough question then becomes why hasn't anyone caught her? There is no easy answer. Ultimately, we are left to speculate on the unknown. One thought is that few anglers fish Camelot Bell in such a way as to maximize their chances of catching a truly large fish. The data analyzed in *High Percentage Fishing* showed that a significant percentage of big fish across the country are caught slowly working a jig across deep water structure during the pre-spawn. My own experience fishing Camelot Bell demonstrates that human nature can make executing on this approach extremely difficult. Fishing the lake is expensive, and a fisherman's natural proclivity is to keep casting to cover as much water as possible in the available time. While this may indeed be a good approach for catching numbers of fish, perhaps even numbers of DD fish, the biggest fish in the lake may require a slower more natural presentation to be fooled.

Mike Frazier with a Camelot Bell DD

A secondary opinion is that fish old and big enough to reach record class size are incredibly wary and difficult to catch. Indeed, there are well-documented cases of big fish in other areas of the country being notoriously hard to catch even after being specifically targeted for prolonged periods of time. However, virtually all these fish were caught eventually, often multiple times. It could also be that the fish has been hooked and broke the angler's line or simply come unbuttoned. While these theories of angler inefficiencies and wise old fish are perhaps plausible, ultimately, I'm left feeling uneasy about their explanatory power. Some of the best fishermen in the world have been plumbing the depths of Bell for over a decade. It seems unlikely to me that a giant fish could have thus far avoided making a mistake.

My own leading theory is that if there is a world record class fish in Camelot Bell, it may well be that the fish feeds almost exclusively at night. We know from John Hopes telemetry studies in other Texas lakes that the largest fish in a given system tend to be nocturnal feeders. I see no reason why a private lake should be any different. Camelot Bell is rarely night fished, and this could explain why fish over 16.5lbs have thus far eluded capture.

The last and least exciting explanation may simply be that she's not there. As perfect a big bass factory as Camelot Bell is, it does have limitations. The ideal temperature for bass growth is between 60-75 degrees. Deviations from this optimal water temperature even for short periods may well adversely affect top end growth. North Central Texas experiences hot summers, and while the winters are mild, temperatures do occasionally drop into the 50s. The temperature stability of coastal California may well be an insurmountable advantage forever putting the record out of reach in Texas waters.

Whether this fact ultimately proves true or not, Camelot Bell remains the jewel of the South. Acre for acre she produces more 10lb fish than any other body of water. In any given year she produces more 15lb fish than most states. When she's on there is no doubt, Bell is the best bass lake in the world. Whether a record fish will be caught remains to seen, but every angler lucky enough to fish the lake can't help but believe the next cast could be the one. What lurks in her depths is pure possibility.

Section IV

Chasing Giants

The Greatest Whopper Ever Told

"I've gone fishing thousands of times in my life, and I have never once felt unlucky or poorly paid for those hours on the water."
-William Tapply

No review of the world of big bass would be complete without a discussion of George Perry and his record-breaking largemouth. What follows is a detailed examination of the man and his fascinating fish tale. In the end, whether you find yourself a believer or not, Perry's fish has set an aspirational mark that has withstood the test of time.

On the morning of June 2nd, 1932, then twenty-year-old George Perry awoke to rain. His father had passed away the previous year, and in the midst of the great depression George had taken on the role of provider for his family. The fields were too wet to plow, so young Perry decided he would go fishing in hopes of providing some much-needed meat for the household. He and his long-time friend, Jack Page, loaded up in Jack's Model T and headed to a small off-the-beaten-path fishing hole called Montgomery Lake, just west of Lumber City, Georgia.

The fishing was slow that day, and around 4 pm George and Jack decided to call it quits. As they rowed George's homemade boat back toward shore, George made one last cast with his Creek Chub Shiner. His lure landed at the base of a cypress tree, and moments later there was a swirl and then a series of explosions on the water. For the better part of ten minutes, he battled the giant and ultimately landed the fish that would pole vault him into the hallowed halls of fishing history. George Perry had landed a 22lb 4oz fish, the heaviest largemouth bass ever recorded.

Ann Landers said, "Bragging may not bring happiness, but no man having caught a large fish heads home through the alley." That quote certainly rang true for George and Jack. While excited about the prospect of an evening fish fry, George could not resist the chance to show off his catch. He and Jack loaded up their beast and headed to the town of Helena, approximately 23 miles to the north. Upon their arrival to town, folks told the pair of a big fish contest being hosted by *Field and Stream* magazine and encouraged them to submit their catch for consideration. The details that followed vary by account but the fish was weighed and measured either at a general store or post office and ultimately certified by a notary of the public. Perry submitted the fish's measurements which eventually led to the fish being certified as the new world record largemouth bass. This record has stood for 85 years.

On the surface, the story of this extraordinary fish tale is very appealing. Perry, a simple farmer with an 8th grade education, and no apparent desire for fame or notoriety stumbles across the holy grail of the fishing world in a backwoods Georgia mud hole. At its core, the account has all the aspects of a legendary achievement that resonates with us all. The problem is, when reviewed in detail, the story is shrouded in controversy and contains all the twists and turns necessary for a mystery novel. In the case of Perry's world record fish, the evidence draws a line between fact and fiction so fine it nearly vanishes.

Much of what we know of Perry's story comes from the many interviews he gave over the course of his life or from the exhaustive research done by his acquaintance and self-appointed historian Bill Baab. Bill was an outdoor writer for the *Augusta Chronical* and spent more than 25 years of his life researching and documenting Perry's story. His book, *Remembering George Perry*, stands out as the authoritative source on the life and facts of George Perry and his record fish. While conducting research for this project, I was fortunate to exchange e-mails with Bill which shed a great deal of light on some of the more confusing aspects of the story. While in the end our assessment of Perry's achievement may vary, I'm grateful to Bill for his insights and the time he took to answer my many questions.

Modern Record Rules

The problem with fishing stories is that they are usually told by fishermen. The sad reality is that the history of fishing is filled with countless examples of well-meaning tall tales and worse yet, unscrupulous individuals who have sought fame and fortune through fabricated deeds on the water. Modern world record rules have emerged as a result of this deception. They aim to standardize the process for documenting big fish so that catches may be fairly evaluated. The exact nature of these rules varies by organization, but there are a few rules they almost all have in common. First, the fish must be hooked in the mouth via a legal fishing method. Next, it must be weighed on a certified scale in front of a witness. Finally, there must be clear photographic evidence of the broad side of the fish. To be clear, these rules in their current form did not exist in Mr. Perry's day. That said, independent of time, these basic rules are common sense guidelines that are required to establish the necessary burden of proof for a world record fish. In a legal sense, defendants are innocent until proven guilty. I believe running with this theme may prove a useful exercise. Let's put Mr. Perry on an imaginary trial to see if we can establish enough evidence to convict him of catching the world record largemouth bass. You be the judge.

Eyewitness Testimony

The first hurdle to cross in demonstrating the legitimacy of the Lake Montgomery beast is to examine eyewitness testimony. From the description of the story, one would expect plenty of this sort of evidence to exist. At a minimum, we should have firsthand accounts of the fish from Jack Page, the notary of the public, and of course George Perry himself. Let's examine them in kind:

Jack Page

Jack Page was George Perry's longtime fishing partner and the only person present when the fish was caught. Unfortunately, Mr. Page disappeared from the face of the earth shortly after the catch occurred. Mr. Baab and many others have spent countless hours searching through census data and area cemeteries trying to prove Jack Page even existed. None have succeeded thus far. In fact, no one other than Mr. Perry has any recollection of Jack Page. Perry's fish gained wide notoriety just two years after the catch when it was declared the new world record. It's plausible, but strange indeed that Page never came forth to give his version of the story.

Verdict: Inadmissible evidence: The bottom-line is there is no firsthand account from Mr. Page. Furthermore, there is no independently verifiable evidence Mr. Page was a real person.

The Notary of the Public

There is no consistent story from Mr. Perry or his family as to who the notary of the public was. George Perry is on record saying the fish was weighed at the general store; however, the official account from the Perry family states that the fish was weighed at the post office across the street. Mr. Baab speculates it was Jesse Hall of Helena, GA the owner of J.J. Hall and Co. General Store, who acted as the signatory who verified the weight of Mr. Perry's fish. However, this speculation ultimately remains just that, as none of the firsthand accounts from Perry actually list the notary by name. Exasperating an otherwise easily resolved riddle, the certified document submitted to *Field and Stream*, which included the name of the notary, was lost in the 1950s when it was loaned to an outdoor writer.

Verdict: Here again, inadmissible evidence. Perry and the man who could have been the notary have long since passed away. Even so, there are no firsthand accounts from any notary, purported or otherwise. It took *Field and Stream* two full years to recognize the Perry fish as a record. This length of time raises questions as to whether or not they had their own doubts.

George Perry

Over the course of his life, George gave dozens of interviews about his catch. Unfortunately, many of these interviews presented contradicting details. Basic facts such as the type of lure, the location of the weigh-in, and whether or not pictures were taken seemed to change with the seasons. In other instances, vital facts which would have helped corroborate his case are never mentioned at all. For instance, Mr. Perry never describes how he measured the length or the girth of the fish. Did he use a ruler, a yardstick, a tailor's tape? While the measuring method may seem trivial, we shall see in a later section it could play a fundamental role in helping to unravel the mystery. The scale, which may have been at the general store, or possibly the post office, was purported to be a 100lb scale which measured weights in increments of ¼ of a pound. Unfortunately, no evidence is ever offered that the scale was certified or double checked for accuracy at the time of the weigh-in. To be fair, at the time these thoughts may never have crossed Mr. Perry's mind as he had no idea just how meaningful his catch would become. It is not my intent in this discourse to personally attack the character of Mr. Perry. However, as we evaluate evidence, I do believe it's important to remember that Mr. Perry was a human and humans are subject to observation error. As evidence of this, I offer up another interesting fact: Mr. Perry was the only person ever to win the *Field and Stream* big fish contest twice. Two years after his record-breaking 1932 catch, he submitted a second fish he claimed weighed in at 13lbs 14 ounces. This time, like the previous time, the depression era farmer received prizes worth roughly $2,000 in today's money and a small amount of notoriety. Below, I have included a picture of Mr. Perry's 13 lb 14-ounce submission.

Verdict: You call it.

Physical Evidence: No physical evidence exists of Mr. Perry's fish. He and his family filleted the fish the same day it was caught and consumed it over a period of several days.

Verdict: No evidence to review.

The Post Office Picture

Shortly after his catch Mr. Perry is on record having said there were no photos of the fish taken. His family account confirms this statement. However, years later, Mr. Perry wrote the manufacturer of the lure he used and indicated pictures did exist. He offered to send in one in exchange for some lures from the company. Creek Chub Lure Company would have obliged the proposal, but never received the photo. Mysteriously, in 2005 a picture of a giant bass emerged which had the potential to provide a mountain of evidence for the giant Georgia bass. In fact, at the time of its discovery, many heralded it as a game changer in favor of Mr. Perry. The photo was discovered by Jerry Johnson of Waycross, Georgia, who claimed to have found the picture in the personal belongings of his deceased aunt, Mildred Johnson. The photo shows a man and a boy with a large bass. While it's impossible to judge the size of the bass in the picture, it is clearly quite large. If you compare it to Mac Weakley's photo of "Dottie" when she was 25lbs, the fish share a very similar body shape. (Next Page) There's no doubt, if the man in the photo could be confirmed to be Perry, the balance might shift. Unfortunately, individuals from the Perry family and Bill Baab himself have confirmed the man in the picture is not George Perry. Perry neither smoked nor drank, and the man in the photo has a cigarette in his mouth. There is some speculation the man in the photo is Jack Page, but the world may never know as no one has

ever been able to positively identify either the man or the boy in the photo. Adding a small amount of authenticity to the photo, there is some genealogical evidence that confirms that the Johnson family and the Perry families were in contact around the 1932-time period. How much this evidence means, however, is impossible to decide as it comes as no surprise that folks from a small rural area of Georgia might be familiar with other families in the area. It should also be noted individuals from the area have stated that the photo appears to have been taken outside the post office in Helena. That said, the detail in the background of the photo is insufficient to be able to prove this claim categorically.

Verdict on the Post Office Photo

This picture proves very little in relation to the Perry fish. The man in the photo is demonstrably not George Perry, and the identities of whoever the individuals actually are is unverifiable. Furthermore, the time and place of the photo cannot be verified, and most importantly, the size of the fish in the photo cannot be confirmed. While it most likely is an authentic photo of a huge fish, we cannot use it as evidence to support the 22lb 4-ounce weight of the Perry fish. It's a tantalizing piece of evidence to be sure, but ultimately it lacks the necessary lineage to prove meaningful. As a final thought, if this was the picture of the fish that Mr. Perry alluded to in his letter to Creek Chub, why didn't he ever bring the image to light? He had countless chances during dozens of interviews.

The Plow Field Picture

There is one other supposed photo of Perry and his fish that significantly adds to the mystery. The picture shown on the next page was sent via e-mail to Bill Baab from a mysterious man on June 2nd, 2013. To readers paying attention, the timing of this e-mail should raise an eyebrow. Paraphrasing a bit, in his book, Baab describes the encounter as follows: The man who sent the photo claimed to be the son of Jack Page and indicated this photo was one of several such photos found in an old tobacco shed in Florida which had been owned by his father. Baab says the man claimed Jack Page had died in the 1950s and

that he and his father were not close. The man also claimed his father had told him growing up that he was, in fact, the man who had caught the record fish and not George Perry. Immediately after that statement, however, the man acknowledged that he never knew when to believe his father. When Bill responded to the e-mail, the man promptly blocked Bill, and disappeared into the ether never to be heard from again. I asked Baab his personal opinion on the existence of Jake Page. He told me he was confident Jack was real, but that Perry had never commented to him directly as to why the friendship had inexplicably dissolved shortly after that fateful day on June 2nd, 1932. Baab said that his working theory on the matter was that there was a falling out over Perry's failure to split any of the prize winnings from the big fish contest. As both men are dead, in all probability this is a riddle that will never be answered. In regards to the picture itself, I asked professional photographer Jonathan Canny, to review the photo. He commented, "The focus of subject and fish appear strange in the photo. Perry's face is clear, the fish looks almost high definition, yet his legs in roughly the same plane are blurred more than one would expect. This could be the result of bad glass in the camera, but it is suspect to say the least. The back of the fish looks as though it may have been altered in a computer program. Lastly, a special setting on the camera would have been required to capture the drops of water falling off the fish. They appear out of focus and blurry, yet the ripples on the water are relatively sharp." In conclusion, Jonathan said,

"To my eyes, the image has been tampered with. I don't think it was done with intent to sell a lie, but rather an attempt to improve the image. I don't believe that it's a spliced image, but I mention it to call attention to the fact that a trick like that was available at the time. People think Photoshop is a new invention of computers, but everything done in Photoshop has roots in methods conceived in the dark room. If I was forced to take a stand on this picture, I'd say that it's an awkward photo taken with a low-quality camera and someone attempted to restore or clarify it at some point."

I myself initially concluded the photo was a fake giving the most weight to the peculiar nature of the fish's mouth. I had never seen a fish posed in this fashion, and frankly, it just looked fake. While researching for this book, much to my surprise, I came across many other photos, virtually all of them from the same period, with fish posed in a similar fashion. Apparently, in the 1930s, this was a common way to pose with ones catch. One of those photos I came across happened to be none other than George Perry. (Next Page) In reflecting on the matter, it seems unlikely to me a modern-day forger would have had the insight to replicate a pose from the period. When I asked Bill Baab about the photo, he told me he was confident the photo was real. He said that Dazy (Perry's son) had positively identified the man as his dad when shown the picture. Bill also commented that he believes the photo had been taken alongside a plowed field a short way away from Lake Montgomery.

As a youngster, George Perry, shown above with a five-pounder, saved his pennies to buy his first fishing tackle. The one lure he could afford landed the world's greatest bass.

Verdict on the Plow Field Photo

I can't say for certain whether the picture of the kneeling Perry and the wide-mouthed bass is a fake. At a minimum, the evidence indicates it's been altered. If it is a genuine photo of Perry and a big bass, I'm intensely skeptical that it is a photo of the world record fish. It appears to be much smaller than 22lbs, and I find it odd that the pair would have brought a camera along on a rainy day when they were simply out fishing for food. Remember, at this time, the nation was still embroiled in the Great Depression, and the pair were so poor that they had only one lure with them and shared a rod and reel!

While it wouldn't prove anything in regards to the record fish, it would certainly be an interesting bit of history if the original copy of this photo ever surfaced and was shown to be real.

Weather/Astrological Evidence

Further examination of the post office photo also casts doubt on the Perry story. All of George's accounts indicate the reason he went fishing the morning of June 2nd, 1932 was that it was raining and the fields were too soggy to plow. The nearest metropolitan area that has weather data available from 1932 is Macon, Georgia. Macon is roughly 100 miles north of Lake Montgomery. Interestingly, it shows there was zero precipitation recorded on June 2nd, 1932. Given its location, however, it's impossible to say if Mr. Perry had his story wrong on the weather of the day. Spotty thunderstorms are common that time of year and could have saturated the Lake Montgomery area and not Macon. That said, while we can't prove the photo of the boy and the man has any ties to Perry, it is worth noting that there are strong shadows in the photo indicating it was likely taken on a sunny day. Here again, this is not definitive proof the fish is not the Perry fish, but it is interesting nonetheless.

There is one final bit of astrological evidence we can derive from the photo which casts further doubt on Mr. Perry's story. The analysis that follows, to the best of my knowledge, has never before been conducted on this photo. The official account documented by Bill Baab on page five of his book indicates Perry caught the fish sometime after 4 pm on June 2nd. Perry said there was at least a 10 minute battle with the beast. After landing the fish and taking care of the boat, George and Jack then drove Jack's Model T 23 miles over dirt roads to the town of Helena. Model T's of the period had top speeds of approximately 30 mph over such terrain. Rough math would indicate the earliest time George and Jack could have possibly arrived in Helena with the fish would have been well after 5 pm Baab himself admits their arrival was "hours after the catch." Interestingly, we can see from the photo that shadows are being cast at a distinct 45-degree angle. Solunar data, available from June 2nd, 1932 indicates that the sun would have been in a position in the sky to create the 45-degree shadow at 3:50 pm. This makes it physically impossible for the fish in the photo to be Perry's, unless of course, like so many of the other details in the story, the time of the catch was reported incorrectly.

Verdict: Weather and astrological evidence cast doubt on the authenticity of Perry's story.

Oddities

Ray Scott, founder of B.A.S.S. ordered Terry Drace, who was one of his employees to interview Perry and conduct a lie detector test. Some accounts of the encounter indicate Drace asked Perry to take the lie detector test and he declined. Bill Baab's version suggests, after interviewing Perry for hours, Drace decided not to ask Perry to take the test. Another oddity in the Perry case is that he never discussed the big fish with his son George (Dazy) Perry. Dazy was 30 years old when George died in a plane crash in 1974. Dazy has expressed great regret about never discussing the topic with his father.

Verdict: It's impossible to draw reliable conclusions from these facts. As a matter of personal opinion, I find it odd that a reporter would defy his boss by declining to ask Perry to take the lie detector test. It seems much more likely that Perry would have been the one to decline. Also, as a matter of opinion, I find it strange that Perry and his son never discussed the fish. One would think such a claim to fame would have been a regular topic of discussion. Was the big fish something Perry was ashamed to talk about to his son?

Biological Evidence

Most damning of all to Perry's story is the evidence of the biological improbabilities of his fish.

Let's review the major points:

The Size of Lake Montgomery

There has been a great deal of confusion about the size of Lake Montgomery. I asked Bill Baab for clarity here, and he informed me that in Perry's day the lake was quite sizable. His best guess was somewhere in the neighborhood of a mile long and perhaps 400 yards wide. The lake was flooded seasonally by the nearby Ocmulgee River. Baab indicated that outside of the flood seasons the lake was typically isolated from the main river. In more recent years the lake has shrunk considerably and is now no more than a few acres and sometimes completely dry.

Verdict: Plausible. The lake in its former size in 1932 could have conceivably supported a large fish. As an interesting side note, I spoke with a big bass biologist from South Texas who told me years ago he would have never believed small lakes could support large fish. However, all that changed a few years ago when he electroshocked a small lake no more than an acre in size. Amazingly, amongst the many fish they shocked up, they found three large bass ranging in size from 6 to 9lbs. After being left in a holding tank during the day, several of the fish regurgitated the remains of multiple blackbirds. These fish had not only survived in a small body of water; they had figured out how to thrive!

The Size of Perry's Fish

One of the biggest strikes against Perry's fish is its purported size. At the time of the catch, there were no other well-documented giant bass to which Perry's fish could be compared. In recent years however, several bass have emerged that threatened Perry's record weight and their length, girths, and weight come well documented. First is the case of "Dottie," the bass famously caught multiple times out of Lake Dixon in California in the 2000s. In 2003 she was caught and weighed in at 21lbs 11 ounces. She was next caught in March of 2006 and weighed in at 25lbs 1 ounce. This weight, incidentally, would have made her the new world record; unfortunately, she was foul hooked making the catch ineligible. When she was finally found dead in May of 2008, she measured 29.5" in length and had a girth of 24". The second big bass data point comes from Manabu Kurita's world record bass out of Lake Biwa, Japan, caught in 2009. His fish weighed 22lbs 5 ounces, technically tying it with Perry's fish for the World Record. Her length was 27.2" and girth 26.7". Both fish are dwarfed by the dimensions reported by Perry at 32.5" in length and 28.5" in girth. Relative to Manabu's bass, Perry claims his bass was 19% longer (32.5") and had a girth 6% greater (28.5") and yet actually weighed in 1 ounce less than Manabu's fish. Unless Perry's bass was made of something *lighter* than bass, this is, of course, a physical impossibility. When I asked Baab about this discrepancy, he noted that the primary forage in Lake Montgomery was bream, and he was unsure of the main forage in Lake Biwa. In Baab's mind, the forage could have perhaps influenced the density of the fish. While I have no definitive proof, I strongly doubt this logic and as it turns out the primary forage in Lake Biwa is also bream. Note: IGFA rules require fish less than 25lbs to exceed previous records by more than 2 ounces to qualify as a new record. Hence Perry and Manabu currently share the World Record.

Further evidence along this thread can be had from statistically derived formulas used to estimate the weight of bass. The first commonly used formula is (LxLxG)/1,200 = Weight. It yields an estimated weight for Perry's fish of 25.1lbs or 12.7% greater than reported 22.25lbs. The other formula widely used is (LxGxG)/800, which yields an estimated weight of 32.9lbs or 48.3% higher than the 22.25lbs Perry reported. The average of these two methods yields an estimated weight of 29lbs or 30% greater than the weight reported. Applying the same logic to Dottie's dimensions, at the time of her death, the estimated weight comes out to 19.3lbs, virtually spot on to the 19lbs observed. Similarly, for Manabu's bass, the average comes out to 20.5lbs, 9% lower, as compared to the actual weight. It's only in the case of Perry's fish the formula breaks down indicating the length and girth dimensions should yield a bass that weighs far more than recorded. The question then becomes, "Which of Perry's measurements were wrong: the length, the girth, or the weight?" It is, of course, impossible to know. What we can state with virtual mathematical certainty however, is that at least one, if not all three of these measurements, were incorrectly reported by Perry.

Genetics

Lake Montgomery is beyond the natural range of Florida-strain bass. There is no evidence to suggest Florida-strain bass were ever transplanted in the Ocmulgee River area prior to 1932. Baab admits as much in his book arguing the fish was a pure northern-strain bass. The largest northern-strain bass ever caught and recorded was less than 16lbs. This would make Perry's fish nearly 40% bigger than any other northern-strain bass ever recorded. Many years after Perry's catch, Florida-strain bass were introduced to Georgia, and subsequently bass as large as 18lbs have been documented in the state. However, even compared to the more recent Florida-strain giants out of Georgia, Perry's fish still exceeds the next biggest bass out of the state by more than 20%. If real it would be a statistical anomaly to say the least.

Pre-Spawn in June

In his telling of the story, Perry made it clear, when the fish was filleted it was full of roe. While this could certainly help explain the increased weight of the fish it, also creates a biological problem that casts some additional doubt on Perry's story. While sizable in 1932, Lake Montgomery was by all accounts relatively shallow. In central Georgia average temps in June have highs well into the mid-80s with nighttime lows in the 70s. There is very little doubt the water temperate in the small lake would have been in the upper 70s to lower 80s. Largemouth bass spawn when water temperatures rise into the lower 60s. In central Georgia, the spawn typically begins in early March and in late years may extend into mid-May. Biologically speaking, Perry's fish being pre-spawn in June would be an outlier but perhaps not unheard of. It is noteworthy that no other bass caught in North America which cracks the top 25 largest bass list, has been caught outside of the southern spawn months of February to May.

Verdict: While some of the biological evidence can be explained away, other aspects of the story, particularly the reported weight and dimensions of the fish, are demonstrably false. The genetics don't pan out, and the measurements don't add up. I ask the reader, "What is more likely: a bass that defies physics, or a fisherman who has made a mistake in measurement or perhaps stretched the truth?"

Closing Commentary:

Famed big bass expert Doug Hannon, dubbed "The Bass Professor," vehemently argued the Perry fish was a false record. He concluded the fish was either a Striped Bass native to the river system that was misidentified or that the fish likely weighed a maximum of 13lbs. While it's purely speculation, my best guess is that Perry did, in fact, catch a giant bass. Perhaps the fish weighed well into the upper teens. Such a fish might have a length in the upper 20s" and a girth of 23" or more. If Perry then incorrectly measured the length of the fish by including its curvature (a mistake easy to make with a tailor's tape) he may well have arrived at a length in excess of 30". This coupled with a scale that could have been poorly calibrated or simply misread could have led to a record that never was. Whatever the case, there is overwhelming evidence the fish's dimensions as purported by Perry are a biological impossibility. In our imaginary court case, where we have attempted to convict Perry of having caught the World Record bass, we must acquit. Reasonable doubt abounds in virtually every detail of this whopper of a story. If extraordinary claims require extraordinary evidence, we are left wanting of even the most basic proof. I suspect that deep down Perry knew this all along, but sometimes stories get told and retold so often that eventually fact and myth freely mix. When this happens, the truth of a story may be lost forever, even to the teller.

Big Bass Lessons

"Over the decades of my wage-earning work as a journalist, I would, in times of particular drudgery, I'd push away from my desk and confide to my coworkers that I was on the brink of abandoning not only my job but my home, community, and my entire life's routine. Asked what I would do and where I would go, I would say with considerable conviction that I would start over on some island in the Caribbean set at the center of the finest fishing waters on the planet. 'I will,' I told my listeners, 'spend my days in a small boat afloat on a crystal sea where fish flash bright greetings under a tropic sun.' 'Yes, that sounds fine,' those skeptics would reply, 'but how long do you think you can do that before you get bored?' And my answer was always the same. 'I'll try it for twenty-five years, and then take a second look." -John Cole

Dr. Joe Lambert with a giant

In closing this book, I thought it wise to provide you with the Cliffs Notes. Soak these up while you are soaking a line:

Lessons Learned

-Outside of the pre-spawn/spawn period, shallow pressured water is a poor producer of big bass. Big fish become nocturnal feeders to avoid daytime shallow water pressure.

-In pressured waters, outside of the spawn, big bass are almost always within a 100 yards of deep water. Deepwater is relative depending on the lake but 8 feet or greater is a good rule of thumb for most natural lakes and reservoirs. Knowing this should allow you to rule out large portions of many lakes.

- In the summertime thermoclines develop on many lakes between 15 and 20 feet; below the thermocline, oxygen content is generally too low to support fish life. Lastly, angler effectiveness is dramatically reduced at depths greater than 20 feet; very few lures work well at these depths.

-Outside of the spawn, anglers should target structure/cover in areas between 6-14 feet for big bass.

-The largest bass in any system are primarily nocturnal feeders. If your goal is to catch a new personal best, there is very little you could do to up your odds more than fishing at night.

-Giant bass are rarely found in heavy weed cover. It's too easy for prey fish to hide in, thus reducing the feeding efficiency of big fish. The biggest fish in a system generally prefer sparse cover near significant structure.

-Big bass prefer hard bottoms. Rock bottoms, particularly near transitions from soft to hard bottoms, can be hot spots. Offshore rock piles can also attract big bass. If these places are well known, be sure to check them out at night. Invest the time to learn how your depth finder works. Virtually all of today's models can help anglers decode bottom composition. On many units, red bottoms tend to be softer and yellow bottoms tend to be hard. Areas that transition from red to yellow, particularly if rock piles are present, are worth exploring further.

-Whether fishing in the day or at night, a stealthy approach is an extremely important factor in increasing success rates with big fish. There are many well-documented cases of big fish being spooked by boat noises, electronics, and starts and stops of trolling motors. Very often the best method for targeting big fish haunts is to drift over the area with your electronics off or to anchor.

-Live bait use can be a dominant big fish tactic, particularly if you are confident you have located a small area that holds big fish with sparse enough cover to effectively work the lure. Shiners and crawfish are great options; however, if I was forced to pick just one live bait to use for big bass, I would not hesitate to choose waterdogs. Giant bass find these creatures irresistible.

-Rules of thumb for private water fishing can be quite different from the guidelines for public water. My own research has shown categorically that on public water the best times to fish are low light periods, especially those around morning and evening. On a per hour basis, catch rates are generally 3 to 4 times higher during these periods than other times of day. However, on lightly pressured private water, these peak feeding periods can be remarkably different. While I do not have an expansive data set on private water catches, my observation and the insights I have gathered from folks like Mike Frazier and Gary Schwarz, strongly indicate that in lightly pressured lakes Florida-strain bass prefer to feed during the warmest part of the day. Camelot Bell famously has its best bite window between 11am and 3pm. On most public water lakes, this period tends to have the lowest catch rates on a per hour basis.

-If you asked me whether I'd rather know a big fish location or the hot bait for a particular lake, I'd prefer to take the big fish location 100% of the time. You cannot catch fish that are not there, thus location is far more important to big fish success than the lure. Furthermore, we know from *High Percentage Fishing* and John Hope's studies that big fish have small home ranges. Once you find a big fish, you've essentially found where she lives. There is a fairly limited number of big fish baits that can be used effectively across much of the country. Locate the spot and you can catch the fish with these lures.

-Big baits are not a requirement for big bass. I was once musky fishing a lake in northern Wisconsin that had a well-known largemouth bass population. I threw an enormous musky topwater bait for an entire day. Right before dark I had a massive explosion on the lure and I wound up landing a bass just shy of 6lbs. For a lake within an hour's drive of the upper peninsula of Michigan, I have strong reason to believe that fish was the largest bass in the lake. However, in a lake full of bass, that was my only bass bite of the day. There is no doubt that big baits produce on average bigger fish on a per-bite basis; however, your number of bites will dramatically decrease. This may be desired if you are catching a large number of smaller fish. If this is the case however, I would suggest that the angler is likely fishing the wrong spots on the lake. Big bass spots do not tend to have a high concentration of fish. Large baits do have a time and a place, but many giant bass have been caught on the smallest of worms. You're much better off throwing smaller baits in a known big bass location than you are throwing a large bait randomly across a lake.

- All lakes and regions within the country go through cycles. In fact, the best lakes are much like stocks. By the time the masses know they're hot, it's probably too late to get in on the action. Chasing the latest lake fads is a fool's game. A dominant strategy is to learn a quality lake and fish it hard. If the waters support Florida-strain bass, you can bet they have lunker potential.

*A few notes on the following section: I do not have any affiliation with any rod, reel, or lure companies and where possible I try to avoid calling out specific brands. In some cases, however, this is unavoidable in an effort to provide anglers with the clearest possible information.

Big Bass Lures

Every year there are giant bass caught on virtually every lure classification you can think of. In 2017 a 10lber was caught in Texas on a Chicken McNugget. There are no magic lures that always produce big fish, but statistically speaking there are dominant baits. The following section focuses on a few big fish lures I believe all fishermen serious about chasing big bass should strive to master. Throw these at the right time, in the right lake, in the right spot, and you'll be well on your way to a trophy class bass.

Worms/Lizards

Statistically speaking, worms and lizards account for more big fish on an annual basis than any other lure. The reason for this is multi-fold. First, these lures are some

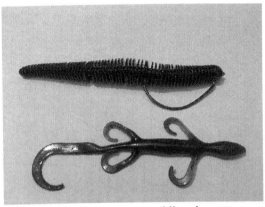

Example worm and lizard

of the most effective bed fishing lures out there, and as such account for many of the giants caught during the spawn. Secondly, these lures have a high hook to land ratio, giving an edge to even novice big fish anglers. Finally, these lures are lifelike enough that fish do not seem to become conditioned to them. After heavy fishing pressure, big bass can quickly learn to associate negative experiences with many other lure classes, such as spinnerbaits. The sounds and vibrations made by these lures are distinctive enough that bass can learn they are not food. This does not appear to be the case with soft plastics as my research has shown that catch rates on these lures have increased over the past twenty years while angler use also continues to climb.

- When to Use Them

Worms and lizards catch fish year-round in many locations. However, they reach peak big bass effectiveness in the months of March-May. This period may be extended into June in northern portions of the country.

- Lure Size

The preferred lure size for big bass can vary widely by the body of water and time of year. Generally speaking anglers too often err on the side of selecting too large of lures. If you are fishing a new body of water where you do not have information of preferred bait size for bass in the lake, start out with 5"-6" lures. If you are getting a lot of smaller fish, size up from there. If you are night fishing, start with larger, bigger bodied lures to increase water displacement, making the lures easier for bass to locate.

- Color

Color matters far less than most anglers believe. Stick with natural greens, browns, and blacks. The one exception is during the spawn when high visibility baits like white may be better options.

- Rigging

Rigging varies by application and fishing conditions. Carolina, Texas, weightless, and pegged rigs are all common. In most shallow water situations during the pre-spawn and spawn Texas rigged lures tend to dominate. Pegged lures allow more precise fishing and fewer missed fish, but may also result in fewer bites as fish may notice the weight on the pickup. In all cases, make sure the hook is unexposed, buried in the plastic, and correctly centered in the bait. Few if any big fish are missed from unexposed hooks; however, countless big fish never bite a lure because it has become fouled with weeds on an exposed hook.

- Hook Size

Hook size is of course contingent on lure size. However, if you are targeting trophy fish, it is highly advisable to use the heaviest wire gauge hooks you can find. A 10lb fish will have little trouble straightening most standard wide gap worm hooks. On Camelot Bell, I used

7/0 owner beast hooks. Even with these giant hooks, I've heard stories of anglers straightening the hook while battling to keep a monster from diving into dense cover.

- Working the Lure

It can't be said enough that for big bass, work your soft plastics slowly. Retrieves can vary from bounces and skips to straight drags across the bottom. Anglers are advised to experiment and determine what the fish want at any particular time. A big bass absolutely will hit a stationary lure on the bottom. Long pauses can sometimes be the key.

- Structure/Cover

When rigged correctly, worms and lizards are essentially weedless and can be fished through most sparse to medium density cover. Snagging can be an issue on rocky bottoms with jagged small to medium sized boulders. These lures may lose some of their effectiveness in heaviest weed cover, which chokes the lure before it reaches the bottom.

- Rod

Use a 7-foot heavy rod with a fast action tip.

- Reel

I recommend a medium to heavy 5:1 gear ratio bait caster. Today's market is flooded with high 6:1, 7:1 even 9:1 gear ratio reels. The key to big bass fishing a worm or lizard is to move the lure slowly. This becomes increasingly difficult to do with the higher ratio reels.

- Line

In clear water environments, 12lb-17lb fluorocarbon will usually generate the most bites. However, if you are fishing heavy cover or targeting truly trophy fish (12lbs +) 65lb braid may be your best option to minimize the likelihood of breakoffs.

> **Lunker Lore:** In most cases, I'm a firm believer that scents do little to improve catch rates. However, in regards to soft plastics being slowly fished in small areas for big bass, I believe the economics of scents may be justified for a slight advantage on big fish. The lizard I used to catch the 10lber on Camelot Bell had been dipped in Chartreuse JJ's Dipping Sauce. Of course, it's impossible to know for sure whether the fish would have bit without the extra scent or color, but I do believe it played a factor. The only true certainty with JJ's dipping sauce is that if you get any on your boat, it'll always be there as a permanent reminder of whether it worked or not!

Squarebills and Deep Diving Crankbaits

Squarebill and deep diving crankbaits combine a compact hard body and an enticing wobble to create an extremely effective big bass bait. Squarebills are most often used early in the season around thick wooded cover and rocky structure. Deep diving crankbaits, on the other hand, shine in the summer months and can probe depths where fish rarely see lures. While these lures can be prone to losing fish through spit treble hooks, every year they account for a sizable number of big bass. The

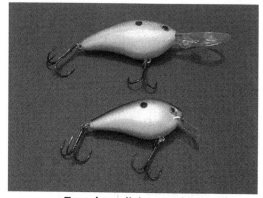

Top: deep diving crankbait
Bottom: shallow crank

key to their effective use is recognizing when conditions are conducive to increased fish activity. Generally, early in the season, this occurs during multi-day warming trends.

• When to Use Them

Squarebill crankbaits can be utilized effectively anytime the water temperature is above 50 degrees. However, their peak period for big bass production is in the pre-spawn period. Deep diving cranks can be used any time of year, but typically do best in the summer months when fish have high metabolic rates and are willing to chase lures actively.

• Size

The KVD 2.0 is perhaps my favorite shallow water squarebill. However, if I'm fishing known trophy waters,

I'll sometimes upsize to the much larger 8.0 squarebill. Deep diving crankbait selection is of course entirely contingent on the desired depth you wish to fish. A KVD 6XD is a great all-around bait for depths up to 17 feet. The larger 10XD is a giant producing juggernaut that can probe even deeper, allowing you to contact fish that rarely if ever see lures!

- Color

Crankbait color selection should aim to match the primary forage in the lake. When in doubt light shad colors produce all across the country.

- Rigging

Synch knots, such as the popular Fisherman's Knot, can be prone to line burn with fluorocarbon which can reduce effective strength. For this reason, a Palomar Knot is highly recommended in crankbait applications.

- Working the Lure

Fishing squarebills is all about contact. The goal should be to thump and bump it off every stump, rock, dock, tree, and root you can find. During the pre-spawn period, fish can still remain lethargic, and the squarebill can generate reaction strikes that other baits simply can't. You will rarely catch fish if you are not bumping and smashing them into cover. Their action, buoyancy, and bill design make them perfect for this task, but you will get hung up from time to time. Take an aggressive mentality and don't be afraid to get the bait hung up. Repetition can be another key factor when fishing a squarebill early in the season. If the area is a known big bass haunt, don't be afraid to throw to the same target multiple times. If the fish are not actively feeding, this repeated and erratic motion from the bait can trigger a reaction strike.

Deep diving crankbaits shine in the summer when many baitfish have relocated to cooler deeper waters. These deep-water haunts often remain the least pressured on many bodies of water making them prime targets for big summertime bass. When fishing deep diving crankbaits, the key is making sure the lure is making contact with the bottom. All baits run different depths depending on line diameter, retrieve speed, and underwater currents. Cast the lure over a large flat of known depth and make careful note of the depth at which the lure stops making bottom contact. This should be the maximum depth in which you use the lure. From here use the lure along the outside edge of deep weedlines, parallel to steep drop-offs and rocky points, and over offshore hard bottom humps and feeding benches.

Both squarebill and deep diving crankbaits can benefit from erratic retrieves. Short random pauses and retrieve speed changes can often trigger strikes. Steady retrieves will produce many fish, but feel free to experiment to see if subtle changes trigger more bites under specific conditions.

- Structure/Cover

Crankbaits excel anywhere weed growth is sparse enough to allow the lures to be effectively worked. They are particularly effective around timber and rock.

- Rod

Squarebill crankbaits are best fished on a 6'8" to 7'0" crankbait rod. A slightly shorter rod allows for more control and increased accuracy in presenting the bait into heavy cover. Deep diving crankbaits are best fished with 7'+ glass crankbait rods to maximize casting distance.

- Reel

High gear ratio bait casters are generally desired when fishing crankbaits. The 6:1 ratio is perhaps the all-around best. In cold early season waters, anglers should be careful not to fish these lures too fast.

- Line

Squarebill crankbaits are designed to be crashed through thick cover. Heavy lines are required to accomplish this. Fluorocarbon in the 12-20lb range works best to get the baits as deep as possible while also minimizing the chance of line breaks. The name of the game for deep diving crankbaits is to get them down as deep as possible. To work effectively these lures need to be digging up on the bottom on the retrieve. The thinner the diameter fluorocarbon, the deeper these lures will get.

Here the angler has to balance a desire for depth with the ability to pull big fish from cover. For most applications, 12lb-17lb fluorocarbon will work best.

> **Lunker Lore:** Add a circular split ring to each hook to create additional action on the bait and to allow more degrees of freedom for hook movement. This will lower angular stress on the hooks when reeling in fish resulting in fewer bent hooks and fewer lost fish.

Jigs

The jig is a highly versatile lure that can be used in a variety of scenarios. It is a spot-on imitation for crawfish, which are one of the top natural forages in lakes from coast to

Black and blue jig

coast. Jigs are especially effective during the pre-spawn period in warmer southern waters as crawdads are emerging from the wintering areas on the banks to take up residence on rocky structures in the lake at the same time big bass are beginning to stage on those same structures. While worms and lizards account for the most fish caught over 10lbs annually, jigs are a close second and regularly produce some of the biggest fish caught each year.

- Jig Options

Jigs come in a wide variety, but the three primary forms are flipping/casting, football, and finesse jigs. Flipping/casting jigs tend to have a larger profile and work well through cover. Football jigs have a large head that balances the lure on the bottom and stand the trailer upright. These lures excel in deeper water rocky and hard bottom applications. Finesse jigs are similar to flipping/casting jigs but tend to have a smaller profile and work well in clearer or more pressured lakes where more subtle presentations may be required. Hook guards should be selected based on the type and density of cover the lure is being worked through. Guards of any sort can and do cause a small number of missed hooksets; however, unguarded jigs can be extremely prone to weed fouling and becoming snagged in rock or wood. In all but the cleanest of lake bottoms, it's wise to fish a jig with some sort of cover guard.

- Trailer Options

In early season cold water applications avoid overly aggressive trailers. Stick to less dynamic trailers that don't create an excessive amount of movement. Once the water warms, virtually all trailer options will catch fish. While nighttime fishing, chose bulky trailers which move a lot of water as the jig is worked back to the boat.

- Color

As with worms and lizards, any natural colors will produce fish. However, studies have shown that black and blue jigs produce a disproportionately large percentage of all big fish caught on jigs.

- Working the Lure

Pitching, flipping, swimming, or crawling are effective methods to fish a jig. Jig fishing expert Logan McKenzie had this to say about jig fishing tactics:

> Pitching –To pitch the jig with a baitcaster, let out enough line so the jig is hanging just above the reel. In a perfect scenario, anglers using a right-handed reel should be pitching with their left hand (and vice versa for a lefty), so they don't need to switch hands once the bait is pitched. With the rod in one hand and the jig in the other, select a target anywhere between 10 and 50 feet away. Use an outward rolling motion with your wrist to create the momentum that propels the jig toward your target. As you start to create the rolling motion, release the jig from your other hand, and allow it to glide toward your target. The key to a good pitch is a smooth rolling motion where you never lose contact with the jig. Do not use your arm to try and propel the bait. It's all in the wrist! It is always a good idea to pitch beyond your target by several feet when possible, as the bait will move forward as you lift your rod tip. A lot of jig bites occur on the initial fall so you must be ready immediately as the bait makes contact with

the water. When this happens, the line often goes slack, as the fish has grabbed it before it has hit the bottom.

Swimming – Swim jigs are a slight variation on traditional flipping and pitching jigs. They usually have a more conical shaped head and are made to be fished in and around vegetation. The conical shape streamlines the bait and allows it to move through grass and other vegetation. A single tail grub is a popular addition to a swim jig.

Crawling – another useful method for fishing a jig is called crawling. This is best done on ledges and points where hard bottom and rock is present. The jig should be cast as far as possible and given a chance to get to the bottom. At the point, it should be reeled/crawled in at a slow pace that allows the bait to barely tick the bottom.

Many of the best big bass anglers agree that crawling is the best approach for trophy fish. The key is to work the lure back to the boat slowly. Retrieves should often be one-half turn followed by a pause. If the jig gets more than 6 inches off the bottom, it will lose virtually all of its big bass effectiveness. In California, it's not uncommon for trophy anglers to make hundreds of these slow retrieve casts to essentially the same area before they are rewarded with a monster bite.

- Rod

    Use a 7ft+ or longer, medium heavy or heavy casting

rod with a fast action tip.

- Reel

In areas with sparse cover low geared 5:1 baitcasting reels work best to ensure the lure is not worked too fast. However, in thick cover high-speed 6:1 – 7:1 gear ratios may be preferred to allow anglers to take up large amounts of line per crank to quickly remove fish from heavy cover they may otherwise become tangled in.

- Line

17lb – 25lb fluorocarbon line or heavy braid work best in most applications.

- Structure/Cover

Jigs excel around wood cover, rocks, and boat docks. They are generally poor selections for weedy areas as they have exposed hooks which can quickly become fouled.

> **Lunker Lore**: Hair jigs are a highly guarded secret of many of the best big bass fishermen. Hair jigs were very common decades ago, but their use has become increasingly rare with the proliferation of plastic skirts and trailers. Anglers would be wise to add these lures to their arsenal, as hair has a natural movement and texture which is impossible for synthetic material to replicate.

Soft-Bodied Swimbaits

Statistically speaking, swimbaits account for a small portion of the lunkers caught in a given year. That said, I believe these baits intimidate many anglers and are likely underrepresented by the data in their ability to produce. If you're going to add a wildcard lure to your lineup, it's hard for me to argue with the big fish potential of swimbaits.

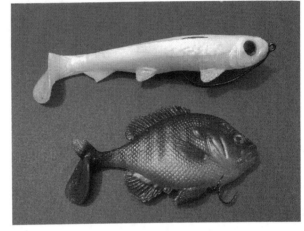

Swimbait examples

The origin of modern swimbaits is murky, but many agree the first appreciable use occurred in California by famed big bass angler Bill Murphy. In 1975 Bill modified a CD18 Rapala by cutting it in two and adding a soft plastic back half that was colored to resemble a trout. He then worked the lure through the depths of San Vincente Reservoir and landed the largest single day 5 bass limit of 72lbs ever recorded in history. If swimbaits didn't have your attention before, they should now!

• When to Use Them

Swimbaits are one of the closest representations of

the forage fish bass naturally feed on that are available in today's market. They are best fished in clear to slightly stained water. The baits are so natural that they create minimal sound or vibration and thus can be difficult for bass to locate in heavily stained or muddy water. The lures can be worked effectively in a variety of situations from deep water structure to shallow weedlines. These lures catch the most fish in water temperatures above 50 degrees but shine in the pre-spawn and spawn periods.

- Color

Select swimbaits that closely resemble the forage fish present in your target area. This obviously varies from lake to lake, but can also vary significantly when fishing different portions of the same lake. A bluegill colored swimbait may be appropriate fishing the outside edge of an 8-foot weedline, while a shad-colored bait may do much better fishing an offshore hump in 18 feet of water.

- Size

As with color, swimbaits should be sized to match the average size of local forage. For giant bass, preferred sizes are often in the 6 to 9-inch range.

- Working the Lure

The key to fishing a swimbait is to make the presentation as natural as possible. As with any lure anglers are advised to experiment, but more often than not, a slow steady retrieve, particularly if fishing deep structure, is the best approach to triggering strikes from monster bass. Anglers are advised to make long casts and to count the lure down to the desired depth. One second per desired foot of descent is a good rule of thumb. Following Tom Young's advice, where possible, fish the lures uphill to provide bass with a unique angle and to increase the odds you'll see follows as the rising bottom will push bass up in the water column where they are more easily seen.

- Structure/Cover

In clear water swimbaits work well in most big fish structures. Funnels, saddles, rocky points, and offshore humps are all great locations. In heavy cover, the lures can be fished weedless. Many varieties can be burned through shallow cover on weightless hooks, or slow rolled over deep structure on weighted hooks.

- Rod

Medium heavy to heavy 7'+ rods.

- Reel

Use large capacity baitcasters to facilitate long casts. Speeds will vary depending on season and water temperature. Generally, slower geared reels will help keep anglers from fishing the baits too fast.

- Line

Swimbaits work best in clear water. Heavy

fluorocarbon in the 17-20lb range is recommended to get the lures deep but also reduce the risk of losing expensive lures on hang-ups in cover.

> **Lunker Lore:** Beyond their big-bass-catching ability, perhaps the most valuable thing swimbaits bring to the table is information. More than any other lure in the bass fisherman's box, swimbaits generate follows. This is especially obvious in clear water settings. With his tracking studies, John Hope taught us big bass are creatures of habit with relatively small home ranges. Half the battle is discovering these locations. Simply put, follows allow fishermen to learn where big bass live even if they don't get a strike. If you do get a follow but no strike from a quality fish, mark a waypoint on your electronics. Return during low light periods (sunrise/sunset) with another high percentage lure such as a jig or worm.

Hooksets, Landing, Weighing and Handling

Hook sets should be hammered home hard as soon as a bite is felt. Big fish can have tough mouths, and the heavy gauge wire hooks can require more pressure than their smaller counterparts to penetrate. Once hooked, single hooks used in most worm/lizard applications have the highest landing percentage of any lure, often more than 90%, in the hands of skilled anglers. Treble hooks have the lowest landing percentage of big fish lures, with landing rates often running in the 75% range. Regardless of the lure type, it's always best to keep rod tips low, even sub subsurface if necessary to discourage a big fish from jumping. As most anglers are keenly aware, the jump creates the highest probability of a fish being able to shake loose a hook. There are two schools of thought on how to land a big fish. The first states that it's best to play the fish out; the other is that big fish should be landed as quickly as possible. I'm a firm believer that landing big fish as fast as possible is a statistically superior approach. The reality is the longer big fish are on the line, the higher the probability something goes wrong. If you are specifically targeting big fish you should have on heavy line, heavy gauge hooks, and a net readily available. Get the fish boat-side as quickly as possible, and position the net in the water facing the direction the fish is coming. Go to great lengths to avoid changing the direction of the fish. Attempting to turn the head of the fish to get it into a poorly positioned net can lead to last-minute heartbreak when the change in direction works a hook loose.

Poor handling of big bass can be fatal far more often than most anglers might think. Big bass are different creatures. Their own weight makes it very dangerous to their health to be handled and weighed. The lower lip hold that works great for smaller fish can easily dislocate or break the jaw of a giant bass. Once in the net, anglers should first wet their hands before touching the fish to avoid damaging their slime coat. Careful attention should be exercised to support the fish's weight at both the mouth and the body. Always maintain at least two points of contact to avoid dropping the fish and overstressing a single point on the body. Weighing the fish is best done with a "Boga grip" style scale that is calibrated and designed to handle fish safely. Attach the grip to the top jaw of the fish and hold the fish close to the ground to minimize damage should it flop and come free of the scale. Weighing large bass through the outer gill plate or by poking a hole through the lower jaw is dangerous to the fish. Contacting a gill could easily kill the fish, and creating a sizable hole in the mouth tissue creates an additional opportunity for infection. If you plan to get measurements do so on a bump board and avoid laying a fish down on carpet, which will remove its protective slime layer. After a quick weight and measure, it's now time for the picture.

The Art of a Big Fish Picture

Most folks have never seen a giant bass over 10lbs up close and personal before. Even for those who have, most have not seen many. It is therefore exceedingly difficult for even expert anglers to accurately judge the size of a fish by a picture. That doesn't stop most of us from trying though.

Here's a tale of two big fish. Before reading further, take a minute and try to guess the weight of each fish on the next page.

> **Lunker Lore:** Instead of still photos consider posing and having a friend use a cell phone to video you and your fish. You can go back later and take screen shots maximizing your chances of getting a great looking picture.

Most would agree the fish on the right looks significantly larger. It turns out the first fish is a 13lber and the second just over 8.5lbs. The difference between the two is much more than 5lbs; it's the fine art of taking a great big fish picture.

There's an old debate about whether it's the dress that makes the woman, or the woman that makes the dress. The same can be said of pictures of giant bass. You can have a true monster, but if you get a bad picture, you'll be forever defending the honor of your trophy to your skeptical buddies. With these thoughts in mind let's examine a few picture taking strategies that can help make your giant look to others way she did when you pulled her out of the water.

If we look at the picture of the 8.5lber, one of the first things that stands out is that the fish itself takes up about

80% of the entire horizontal frame of the picture. This effect can be achieved in three primary ways. First, the angler extends his arms to make the fish appear large against the backdrop of his body profile. Next, the photographer is close enough to the fish that it fills the majority of the frame. Finally, the fish is held horizontally which maximizes the perception of length.

Next, the individual is sitting down which makes the fish occupy a significant portion of the frame vertically as well. This is an often-overlooked tactic that can make a huge difference. The angler is also careful to position his hands in such a way that they are barely visible. This maximizes the perceived size of the fish. As icing on the cake, the angler also positions the fish perfectly to ensure the degree of bend in his arms is not discernable. Perhaps most impressive he does all this with a smile. Well played sir, well played.

Here are a few additional tips for a healthy release. Be sure to support the weight of large fish with the use of both hands while raising them from the water and posing for a picture. There have been many instances of delayed mortality of fish that get broken or dislocated jaws from well-meaning anglers. As fish approach or exceed 10 pounds, this risk becomes exponentially greater. Do whatever you can to minimize the time the fish is out of the water. Remember they cannot hold their breath any longer than you without suffering possible harm. Whenever possible, it's best to keep fish out of the water for no longer than 30 seconds. Finally, make sure you prep your photographer on all these important concepts prior to removing the fish from the water. At the end of the day, perhaps the most important aspect of the perfect picture is achieving it quickly to ensure a healthy release.

I'm not advocating a form of photographic deception by making 5's look like 10's through full arm extension and a picture taken so close the lens is wet afterward. Good anglers will see right through this charade. All that said, I do not believe there is anything wrong with a natural and moderate extension of the arms coupled with a few wise photographic strategies. You and your bass had a date with destiny that was a lifetime in the making; don't sell either of you short.

Closing

Over the course of writing this book, I had the great fortune of speaking with many of the best big bass anglers alive. Much to my surprise, perhaps the most pervasive trait amongst them was a profoundly humble spirit in retelling their angling achievements. Salesmen, doctors, biologist, giants of industry— more often than not they had all been laid low by fish. Odell Shepard said it like this, "In other arts and crafts and even in a few sports, we can distinguish the three stages of apprentice, journeyman, and master; but in angling few ever pass beyond apprenticeship and masters, there are none."

I began my hunt for big bass in January of 2016 while

living in Houston, Texas. In September of that same year, a job change required me to relocate my family to Wisconsin leaving behind some of the best big bass water in the country. However, during those nine short months, applying the lessons I learned and fishing no more than once or twice per week, I landed 22 bass over 5lbs and six fish between 7 and 9 pounds from public water. On my first trip to Camelot Bell, I crossed the magic double-digit threshold and landed a beautiful 10.5lb giant. Some may find this private water accomplishment unimpressive, but I'm proud of that fish, and the knowledge I acquired catching her. I fished smart and hard during my time in the South, and I emerged transformed. Big bass fishing is addictive to be sure. It can consume your thoughts and haunt your dreams. I miss southern water dearly, but I've been able to apply the same lessons here in Wisconsin targeting the biggest bass in the local systems with great success.

    It's my sincere hope that something in this book has resonated with you and will improve the size of fish you're catching. I also hope that it sparks in you a desire to head out on the water and see what's possible. As for me, I set out on my big fish adventure with the intent of catching a fish of a lifetime. Some will ask whether I have achieved this goal. In reflection I can't help but think— of course not. I've only just begun.

Lunker Lore

1. Fish where big bass live
2. Fish the pre-spawn and spawn periods
3. Fish known big fish haunts, funnels, feeding benches, rock piles
4. Fish low light periods (morning/evening) and at night
5. Look for stability in weather
6. Live bait and anchoring as big bass tactics
7. Avoid heavily pressured areas
8. Avoid cold muddy water
9. Avoid excessively weedy areas
10. Look for hard bottoms

Acknowledgments

Ken Addington: Ken is an incredible fisherman and a kind soul to whom I am incredibly grateful. Without Ken's willingness to share, this book would not have been possible.

Justin Furnace: Justin is one of the most interesting characters I've ever met. He is a force of nature on the water, in the field, and in business. I can't thank him enough for his tactical coaching.

Dr. Joe Lambert: Joe doesn't speak often, but when he does I listen intently as there is always a nugget of invaluable information to be learned. Thank you, Joe, for allowing me to use your many big bass pictures which are scattered across this book!

Mike Frazier: Mike probably knows more about big bass than anyone alive. I'm grateful for his hospitality, the many texts and pictures, and his willingness to share the best bass lake on the planet, Camelot Bell.

Dr. Gary Schwarz: I can't thank Gary enough for taking time he didn't have to talk to me at length about his unbelievable project. His thirst for knowledge will eventually benefit us all!

Tom Young: I've never met Tom, but he's shared an enormous amount of information with me with no pretense at all of getting anything in return. He's one of the best and last of a generation of fishermen who were there at the beginning of the California big bass gold rush. Thank you for sharing, Tom.

Bill Baab: I appreciate Bill taking the time to answer my many e-mails. Bill has likely forgotten more about George Perry's World Record than most of us will ever learn!

John Hope: I thank John for taking the time to sit down with me and discuss his findings; I also thank him for being an inspiration. His tracking studies sparked in my mind a fascination with the science of bass fishing from which I've never looked back.

The Motley Crew: Zach, Andy, Jared, and Craig. I've been fishing with you guys for close to 20 years. Most of the new equipment I have is due to one of you guys breaking my old stuff. In 20 years I don't think I've learned a single thing from any of you, but it's been a ton of fun. Mostly.

Logan McKenzie: Logan is a longtime friend, walking big bass encyclopedia, and the best pure fisherman I know. We've chased big fish all across the country, and I've always learned something from him. From content review to countless hours kicking around ideas, Logan has always been there to help. I appreciate you sir.

Great Websites and Apps

Texas Fishing Forum: The best gathering of fishing minds I've come across. Some great people as well. I consider you guys like family. www.texasfishingforum.com

Western Bass: If you are talking West Coast angling, check out these guys. www.westernbass.com

Bass Resource: One of the best collections of big bass wisdom on the web. www.bassresource.com

Navionics: This boating app for iPhone or Android is top notch. It includes detailed topographical maps for most lakes across the country. It's a must-have for all anglers.

Wind Alert: The best app I've come across for accurate up to date wind forecasts.

Weather Underground: My preferred weather app.

Bass Blaster: Jay Kumar's Bass Blaster is the best summary out there of what's going on in the world of bass fishing. www.bassblaster.rocks or on Facebook.

Lunker Lore: Check this site for occasional updates and big fish blogs! www.lunkerlore.com

High Percentage Fishing: Like us on Facebook.

Also by the Author

Envisioned as the "Moneyball" of largemouth bass fishing, *High Percentage Fishing* offers a practical approach to put more fish in your boat. It freely mixes big bass wisdom from some of the world's greatest fishermen, with statistical findings from a vast database of catch information. Part science, part strategy, this book boils down critical concepts into fundamental truths that will help you catch more fish. Learn about:

- Big bass habits and locations
- The impact of weather on catch rates
- The effect of lunar cycles on fishing
- The best and worst times to fish

Engineer and statistician Josh Alwine slices through the data and demonstrates that some of fishing's oldest and most conventional thinking is little more than myth.

About the Author

Josh Alwine is a lifetime fisherman, who currently resides in Madison, Wisconsin with his family. He has a degree in Industrial Engineering from Purdue University, a Master's in Business Administration from Marquette University, and has achieved a Black Belt certification in Lean Six Sigma. He's fished as far south as the West Indies and as far north as Canada chasing a variety of fresh and saltwater game fish.

Made in the USA
Columbia, SC
27 December 2017